SHOOTING HANDGUNS

AN **INTRODUCTORY GUIDE** TO SHOOTING SAFELY & EFFECTIVELY

Gregory M. Wier
& Stephen D. Wier

SCHIFFER MILITARY
4880 Lower Valley Road   Atglen, PA 19310

We would like to thank Robert and Frances Enck at Enck's Gun Barn for encouraging us to write this book and providing the financial support to make it a reality. We would also like to thank our many shooting friends, too numerous to name, whose skill and wisdom helped craft this text. In particular, we would like to thank Andy McCauley for being an invaluable resource pertaining to shooting fundamentals. Special thanks to Keith Kreiser for his input on left-handed shooters. We would also like to thank Mark Booher of Barritus Defense for his knowledge about Israeli training and their mindset.

Thank you to Adam and Eric Wier for their encouragement and attention to detail when reading through various iterations of the book. Thank you to Aletheia Atzinger for reading early drafts of the book and helping to ensure it is as clear as possible.

Designed by Justin Watkinson

Photography by Bob Smith

Type set in Minion Pro/Univers LT Std

ISBN: 978-0-7643-5837-1

Printed in China

Published by Schiffer Publishing, Ltd.
4880 Lower Valley Road
Atglen, PA 19310
Phone: (610) 593-1777; Fax: (610) 593-2002
E-mail: Info@schifferbooks.com
Web: www.schifferbooks.com

For our complete selection of fine books on this
and related subjects, please visit our website
at www.schifferbooks.com. You may also write
for a free catalog.

Schiffer Publishing's titles are available at
special discounts for bulk purchases for sales
promotions or premiums. Special editions,
including personalized covers, corporate
imprints, and excerpts, can be created in
large quantities for special needs. For more
information, contact the publisher.

We are always looking for people to write
books on new and related subjects. If you
have an idea for a book, please contact us at
proposals@schifferbooks.com.

CONTENTS

INTRODUCTION

WHAT IS THE PURPOSE OF THIS BOOK?

This book is designed to help a novice shooter become comfortable with handling and shooting a handgun effectively. People are often afraid of what they do not understand, and the notion of owning a handgun or being around one can be frightening. A firearm is not dangerous by itself; it is merely a tool. The danger comes from how the tool is used. This book is designed to remove the mystery around handguns and firearms, and in doing so, we hope, remove some of the fear that can go along with them.

The book is separated into a collection of chapters designed to familiarize you with how to use handguns safely and effectively. The chapters are as follows.

1. How to safely handle a handgun

Learning how to safely interact with a firearm is the most important thing to learn when familiarizing yourself with firearms. Because of this, it is the first focus of the book. The chapter is framed around three principal safety rules that need to be followed to ensure that no one is hurt in case of an accident. If you get nothing else from this book, we hope you learn how to safely interact with firearms.

2. Anatomy of a handgun and how it works

In this chapter, the history of handguns is briefly described, chronicling the development of the metallic cartridge, which allowed gun design to advance beyond muzzle-loading weapons such as muskets. The common components of modern firearms are described before specifically describing revolvers and semiautomatic handguns.

3. Ammunition

This chapter discusses all the components that go into making metallic cartridges, the type of ammunition that all modern firearms utilize. A metallic cartridge consists of (1) the bullet, or projectile, (2) a case to hold the gunpowder, (3) the gunpowder, and (4) a means to ignite the gunpowder. Since cartridge naming can be confusing, special effort is taken to describe it. There is no set convention for naming, and the same cartridges often have different names in the United States versus Europe, because the United States has not adopted the metric system. Safety considerations are also explored, along with the topic of loading your own ammunition, which is rapidly becoming more popular due to increasing prices of ammunition.

4. How to choose a handgun

Choosing what to buy when purchasing your first handgun can be difficult, particularly due to the huge number of options available. This chapter discusses what factors you should consider when choosing a handgun, factors that include how it fits into your hand along with what sort of recoil can be expected from it. Every handgun is designed with a particular job in mind, and being aware of that job will help you decide if it is right for you. With the information in this chapter, you should be able to walk into a gun shop and not be overwhelmed with all the options available to you.

5. Shooting a handgun

The process of shooting a handgun is described in this chapter. It is a fairly simple process to understand, but implementing it properly is not nearly as simple. There are two main tenets for shooting a handgun effectively: (1) present the pistol consistently and then (2) do not move the gun when pressing the trigger. Fully realizing these two things is not easy, since they are affected by a plethora of factors: grip, stance and firearm presentation, sight alignment and sight picture, breath control, trigger control, and follow-through. The importance of each of these things is discussed in detail, along with suggestions about how to properly implement them.

6. Pathway to success

Even with a good grasp of the fundamentals of shooting, you will likely run into problems with implementing all of them properly. This chapter discusses some of the common problems that shooters experience and how to fix them.

NOTE: This book is composed of the opinions of the authors and what they believe to be important. You will not become an expert after reading this book, or after reading any single book on the topic.

HOW TO SAFELY HANDLE A HANDGUN

CHAPTER 1 HOW TO SAFELY HANDLE A HANDGUN

The most important aspect to learn when becoming familiar with handguns, and firearms in general, is how to handle them safely. A lot of the fear that people harbor toward firearms derives from a lack of knowledge about them. Oftentimes, more dangerous than a novice is someone who thinks they are well-versed by virtue of growing up around firearms, and mistakes that shallow knowledge for expertise. A handgun can pose a very serious danger to yourself or others if it is mishandled or put in the hands of a careless individual. With the proper knowledge, and a healthy amount of respect for them, handguns should not be frightening or dangerous.

Just having the knowledge of how to safely handle a firearm is not enough; you have to be prepared to employ that knowledge at all times. This goes hand in hand with treating them seriously and with respect. A firearm is not a toy, nor is it something to be brandished to look "tough." If you are buying a handgun to broadcast your power or importance, you are not treating it with the seriousness that it demands. In a similar vein, posing for "cool" pictures with your handgun and pointing it directly at people or the camera is not respecting it either. Such actions are irresponsible and extremely dangerous, explaining why many indoor shooting ranges have no-photograph policies.

FIGURE 1.1. Handling a handgun safely does not need to be a difficult proposition. If you do not point the handgun at anyone, always treat the handgun as if it is loaded, and keep your finger off the trigger until you are prepared to shoot, no one will be hurt in an accident.

Fortunately, safely handling a firearm is not a difficult process (**figure 1.1**), and it can be broken down into three simple tenets:

1 **A firearm should never be pointed at someone or cross over any part of a person.**

2 **Treat all firearms as if they are loaded.**

3 **Your finger should never be on the trigger until you are ready to shoot.**

While these rules may seem self-explanatory, there are some nuances to each of them that warrant explanation. One of the strengths of this set of rules is that if you fail to meet some of them, so long as you follow even one, no one will get hurt in the event of an accident.

1.1. Rules of Safe Gun Handling

1. A firearm should never be pointed at someone or cross over any part of a person.
You should not point a firearm at someone/something unless you are prepared to shoot them/it. This goes beyond intentionally pointing a firearm at someone. Since handguns are fairly small, it can be easy to unintentionally pass the front of the gun (the muzzle) over a part of yourself or someone else. With a rifle (sometimes called a long gun), it is a simple task to keep the barrel pointed away from yourself due to its length (**figure 1.2**). It is of paramount importance that you are always mindful of the facing of the muzzle when you are handling a firearm.

FIGURE 1.2. Since pistols are short and compact, it can be easy to inadvertently point one at someone. Rifles are considerably larger, making it harder to accidentally point one at someone.

Even if you just checked the handgun and know that it is unloaded, you should never point a firearm at yourself or someone else. It takes an instant to load a cartridge into a handgun, and can easily be done by someone else, unbeknownst to you. You want to do everything in your power to minimize damage if the firearm were discharged accidentally. Even if the gun were to go off, if you do not have it pointed at yourself or another, people will not be hurt.

AMMUNITION TERMINOLOGY

There are many different terms thrown around when describing ammunition, making it confusing for someone just getting into shooting. Nearly all modern firearms fire cartridges. A cartridge packages a projectile (the bullet), a propellant (gunpowder), and a pressure-sensitive element (primer) into a metal case. Cartridge is not the only acceptable term; "round" is prevalent as well. It is common to hear cartridges referred to as bullets, though this is a misnomer, since a bullet is just one part of a cartridge.

Beyond being cognizant of yourself and people in your immediate vicinity, you also have to be mindful of your surroundings. Are you handling the gun while inside an apartment? Who might be beyond one of the walls that you are pointing at? How thin are the walls? Depending on the construction of the wall, a bullet could easily pass through. The same goes when you are outside at a shooting range. Where would a shot go if the gun were discharged? Are there suitable backdrops to stop stray rounds? Are there houses in the distance? If you were to shoot into the air, that bullet has to come down and could very easily hit someone. These are all things that you need to be aware of when handling a firearm.

2. Treat all firearms as if they are loaded.

You should always treat a firearm as if it were loaded. This rule is a natural extension of the first rule; just as you would not want to point a loaded firearm at a friend, you should never point an unloaded firearm at them. As was mentioned in the previous point, it is very easy to load a round into a firearm, and it could be done unbeknownst to you. Because of this, the safest policy is to always treat them as if they are loaded.

To go along with this, whenever you pick up a handgun, you should check to see if it is loaded. The most common type of handgun available today is a semiautomatic (**figure 1.3A**; a semiautomatic firearm fires a cartridge every time the trigger is pulled, and uses the energy of the fired cartridge to ready the gun to fire again). A semiautomatic handgun stores its ammunition in a spring-loaded magazine. The magazine holds cartridges, and the spring pushes a new cartridge into place once one is fired. To check to see if a semiautomatic pistol is loaded, you should release the magazine first (**figure 1.3B**) and then pull back the slide to *visually* inspect whether a round is inserted into the chamber of the pistol (the chamber is the rear portion of the gun barrel, where the bullet must be seated to be ready to fire; for additional information about the chamber, see section 2.1). If a round is in the chamber when you pull the slide back, the round will be ejected. To avoid this, you can slowly and carefully pull back the slide partially to reveal a round loaded in the chamber (**figure 1.3C**). If you pull back the slide fully and then release it, it will pick up a new round from the magazine and load it into the chamber as it moves forward, unless you removed the magazine beforehand. This is why you should remove the magazine first when checking a handgun. Make sure to be mindful of the direction the muzzle is facing when you are checking to see whether the handgun is loaded. When you are concentrating on moving the slide and examining the chamber for a cartridge, it can be easy to forget where you are pointing the gun.

Slide
(covers most
of the barrel)   Chamber

Magazine

A

A magazine holding ammunition
inserts into handle

B

FIGURE 1.3. When picking up a handgun, you should always check to see if it is loaded.
A. A semiautomatic handgun holds its ammunition in a magazine that inserts into the handle of the firearm. It is not possible to discern if most semiautomatic handguns are loaded by simply looking at them. A metal slide covers the majority of the barrel of the handgun, leaving only part of the chamber exposed. **B.** When checking to see if a semiautomatic handgun is loaded, you should first release the magazine. This can usually be done with a button on the handle of the gun, often pressable with the thumb of your shooting hand. **C.** After releasing the magazine, slowly pull back the slide partially to see if there is a round in the chamber. The pictured firearm has a round that is being removed from the chamber as the slide is being pulled back.

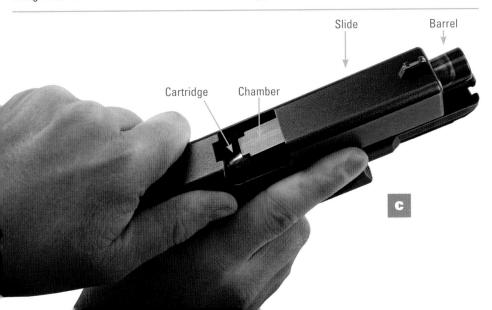

Slide   Barrel

Cartridge   Chamber

C

You may have noticed that "visually" was italicized when describing how to inspect the chamber for a round. It is essential to confirm that the chamber is empty with your eyes. Some people develop the habit of manually pulling the handgun slide back a few times, which should eject any chambered cartridges. If they do not see live rounds being ejected from the gun, they assume it is empty. This is a dangerous assumption. If the extractor on your handgun is defective, it may not eject a chambered round. The only way to be completely sure that the handgun is empty is by confirming it with your eyes. If it is too dark to see inside the chamber, you could put your finger into the chamber and feel for a round. In the instance that your fingers are too large to adequately feel inside the chamber, your best option is to use a flashlight to inspect the chamber for a round.

The importance of checking the chamber of a firearm before handling it cannot be overstated. Even if someone confirms that it is unloaded before handing it to you, you should still check it. Checking the gun yourself is not about distrusting that person; it is about building a safe habit.

3. Your finger should never be on the trigger until you are ready to shoot.

Your finger should never be on the trigger of a firearm unless you mean to shoot it. Some firearms have triggers with very little resistance when pressed (referred to as a "light" trigger pull), such that you could accidentally fire it if your finger is on the trigger. Along these same lines, you could easily shoot yourself in the leg as you draw your handgun from its holster. Rather than having your index finger on the trigger, you should have it straight along the side of the handgun (**figure 1.4**). All commercially available handguns have a loop of metal or polymer surrounding the trigger, called a trigger guard (**figure 1.4A**), which is designed to help prevent accidental discharge. You should find a place that you can consistently place your trigger finger on the frame of the handgun, but it should not be on the trigger guard. Many handguns have some specific geographical feature that can serve as a tactile position to place your finger, but this will be different for every handgun. If you are shooting left-handed, your trigger finger is often lying over the slide stop of the gun (**figure 1.4B**), which can be uncomfortable (the slide stop is a piece of metal that will keep the slide locked back after the last cartridge is fired). Despite the potential discomfort, it is still essential to do,

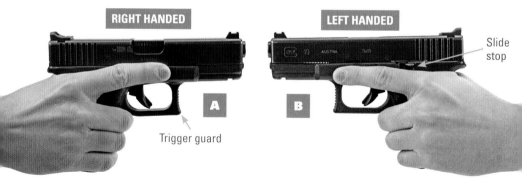

FIGURE 1.4. Your finger should never be on the trigger until you are ready to shoot. **A.** You should have your trigger finger straight along the frame of the firearm, keeping it off the trigger and outside, and away from, the trigger guard. This view is of a right-handed grip on the firearm. **B.** When shooting left-handed, your trigger finger often contacts the slide stop on the side of the handgun. If this feature is pronounced on the firearm, it can be uncomfortable.

since keeping your finger off the trigger is paramount to proper firearm safety. Many newer handguns are designed to be ambidextrous, with all the relevant controls on both the left and right side, but as a general rule, handguns are designed with the assumption that the shooter is right-handed.

One of the simplest tests to determine a person's gun-handling skills is to place an unloaded handgun on a table and ask them to pick it up. If they put their finger on the trigger while picking it up, it is a clear indication they are not familiar with how to safely handle a firearm.

1.2. Use the Proper Ammunition for Your Firearm

While it may seem obvious, it is critical that you check your ammunition before putting it into your firearm. Every firearm is designed to fire a particular cartridge and will not safely fire anything else. Virtually every handgun has the type of cartridge that it fires stamped somewhere on

A

.357 MAGNUM CAL.

FIGURE 1.5. It is essential that you match the proper ammunition with your firearm. **A.** Most revolvers have the cartridges that they fire stamped somewhere on the barrel. The pictured revolver fires .357 Magnum cartridges. The position on the barrel where this is indicated has been highlighted with a yellow box, and that region has been replicated and magnified. **B.** Since the barrel of a semiautomatic handgun is usually obscured by the slide, the cartridge designation is stamped on the slide. The pictured handgun fires 9 × 19 mm Parabellum (9 mm Luger), which is recorded on the slide as 9 mm × 19. The position on the slide where that is indicated has been highlighted with a yellow box, and that region has been replicated and magnified. **C.** Semiautomatic handguns often have the cartridge designation stamped on the exposed portion of the chamber. The pictured handgun fires 9 × 19 mm Parabellum (9 mm Luger). The position on the chamber where this is indicated has been highlighted with a yellow box, and that region has been replicated and magnified.

B

9 mm x 19

C

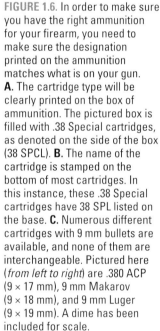

FIGURE 1.6. In order to make sure you have the right ammunition for your firearm, you need to make sure the designation printed on the ammunition matches what is on your gun. **A.** The cartridge type will be clearly printed on the box of ammunition. The pictured box is filled with .38 Special cartridges, as denoted on the side of the box (38 SPCL). **B.** The name of the cartridge is stamped on the bottom of most cartridges. In this instance, these .38 Special cartridges have 38 SPL listed on the base. **C.** Numerous different cartridges with 9 mm bullets are available, and none of them are interchangeable. Pictured here (*from left to right*) are .380 ACP (9 × 17 mm), 9 mm Makarov (9 × 18 mm), and 9 mm Luger (9 × 19 mm). A dime has been included for scale.

the gun. In the case of revolvers, the cartridge is usually stamped somewhere on the barrel (**figure 1.5A**). Most semiautomatic handguns have a slide that covers most of the barrel, so the cartridge type is stamped on the slide (**figure 1.5B**). The cartridge designation is often stamped on an exposed portion of the chamber (**figure 1.5C**) as well. Furthermore, any new handgun will come with an instruction manual detailing this information.

When purchasing ammunition, the cartridge type will be clearly printed on the box (**figure 1.6A**), and it is usually stamped on the head/base of the cartridge (**figure 1.6B**) as well. The name on the cartridge needs to match what is on both the box and the gun. This cannot be stressed enough: the names need to match exactly. Some cartridges have very similar nomenclature, despite being different. As an example, .22 LR (Long Rifle) is not the same cartridge as .22 S (Short), and 9 mm Luger is not the same thing as 9 mm Makarov (**figure 1.6C**). Matching the proper ammunition with the proper handgun is made more difficult by some cartridges being known by multiple names: 9 mm Luger is also known as 9 mm NATO, 9 × 19 mm Parabellum, and more generally as just 9 mm (for more information about cartridge naming, see section 3.2).

Oftentimes, the incorrect ammunition will not fit properly into the chamber of the firearm. However, if the improper ammunition can successfully be loaded into the gun, shooting it is unsafe, since the gun was not designed for it.

Some common cartridges used for defensive firearms are available in increased-pressure variants. These are known as "plus pressure" (+P) rounds and have the same cartridge dimensions as their regular counterparts but have additional gunpowder to make them more powerful. If a cartridge is +P, it will be clearly written on the ammunition box (**figure 1.7A**) and the base of the cartridge (**figure 1.7B**). A firearm

designed to shoot +P rounds will have that stamped somewhere on the gun (**figure 1.7C**). If a firearm is not designed to handle these increased pressures, shooting +P rounds through it could rupture the barrel and cause serious injury (see section 3.3 for further information).

It should be noted that a handgun designed to fire + P cartridges will fire regular versions of the cartridge with no trouble.

FIGURE 1.7. Some cartridges are specifically loaded with additional gunpowder above the standard load to increase the velocity of the round. **A.** If a cartridge is "plus pressure" or "+ P," it will be clearly marked on the packaging. Pictured here is a box of .38 Special (*left*) and a box of .38 Special + P (*right*). **B.** The base of the cartridge will indicate if a cartridge is + P. Pictured here are two regular .38 Special cartridges, one upright and one on its side (*left*), and two .38 Special + P cartridges, one upright and one on its side (*right*). **C.** The pictured revolver is capable of firing .38 Special + P cartridges. The position on the barrel where this is indicated has been highlighted with a yellow box, and that region has been replicated and magnified.

To avoid confusion, it is generally best to load and shoot one gun at a time while at a shooting range (**figure 1.8A**). If multiple handguns are present with different ammunition types, a moment of carelessness could lead to the improper ammunition being loaded into a firearm (**figure 1.8B**).

FIGURE 1.8. Keeping an organized shooting bench is a good way to avoid mixing the wrong ammunition with the wrong handgun. **A.** It is recommended that you limit the number of firearms that you have out on the shooting bench at one time. **B.** The pictured shooting bench is laden with different handguns and the various types of cartridges that they fire. It would not be hard to inadvertently load the improper ammunition into one of the handguns.

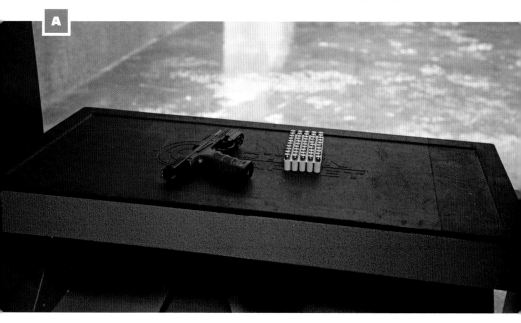

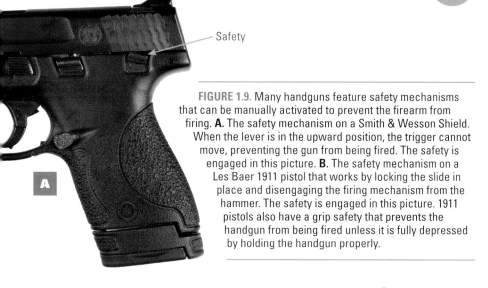

FIGURE 1.9. Many handguns feature safety mechanisms that can be manually activated to prevent the firearm from firing. **A.** The safety mechanism on a Smith & Wesson Shield. When the lever is in the upward position, the trigger cannot move, preventing the gun from being fired. The safety is engaged in this picture. **B.** The safety mechanism on a Les Baer 1911 pistol that works by locking the slide in place and disengaging the firing mechanism from the hammer. The safety is engaged in this picture. 1911 pistols also have a grip safety that prevents the handgun from being fired unless it is fully depressed by holding the handgun properly.

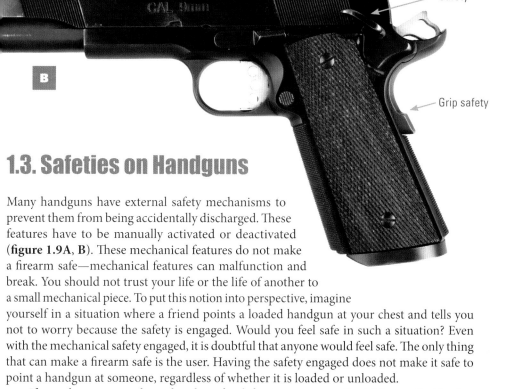

1.3. Safeties on Handguns

Many handguns have external safety mechanisms to prevent them from being accidentally discharged. These features have to be manually activated or deactivated (**figure 1.9A, B**). These mechanical features do not make a firearm safe—mechanical features can malfunction and break. You should not trust your life or the life of another to a small mechanical piece. To put this notion into perspective, imagine yourself in a situation where a friend points a loaded handgun at your chest and tells you not to worry because the safety is engaged. Would you feel safe in such a situation? Even with the mechanical safety engaged, it is doubtful that anyone would feel safe. The only thing that can make a firearm safe is the user. Having the safety engaged does not make it safe to point a handgun at someone, regardless of whether it is loaded or unloaded.

If you plan on concealing a handgun for defensive purposes, it might seem that having a mechanical safety would be important. After all, if you are carrying a gun around on your person, surely you want it to be as safe as possible? While this is true, it is important to remember that a mechanical piece is not what makes a handgun safe; safety comes from how you handle the firearm. There are a number of reasons why having an external safety on a handgun is not ideal for a defensive weapon. If you have to draw your gun in self-defense, time will not be on your side. Adding the extra step of removing the safety will not work in your favor. In the heat of the moment, you will fumble with the safety unless you have practiced with it extensively. Disengaging the safety is something that requires the coordination of your hands and fingers. These "fine motor skills" become compromised under extremely stressful situations, making it difficult to remove the safety unless you are well practiced (for more information about how your body reacts to extreme stress, see section 4.2.4). Furthermore, unless removing the safety has become muscle memory, it will probably require you to momentarily take your eyes off the threat to remove the safety. Because of these things, having an external safety on a concealment gun serves little purpose. Again, the safety feature on a handgun is not what makes it safe; it is how you handle it.

Having a safety can be appealing if you have children in the household, particularly if you plan to have a loaded weapon in the house for home defense. However, that should not take the place of talking to your children about the danger of firearms (for more information about gun safety and children, see section 1.5).

1.4. Storing Firearms Securely

If you are a parent or often have children in your household, you need to take special precautions to ensure that they do not gain access to your firearms. While this may seem obvious, it deserves special emphasis. Children are very resourceful and are persistent enough to access things you may have thought were beyond their reach. Not only do you want to keep your firearms out of the hands of children, you want to keep them away from intruders and thieves. Some states have laws that require gun owners to store their firearms safely when not in use. These laws differ from state to state but often mandate that firearms are stored in a locked container when not in use, or that they are disabled with a gun lock. It is your responsibility to be aware of state and local laws pertaining to gun storage.

What constitutes the best way to store a firearm is up for debate, and it varies greatly on the basis of who you live with. If you have young children in the house, you need to expend serious effort to make sure your firearms are inaccessible. Unfortunately, the most secure and safe gun storage solutions do not lend themselves to quick retrieval in an emergency. A handgun locked away in a gun safe is not easy to retrieve in the dark, while a loaded gun by your bedside is easy to access but poses a significant risk to other people. Below are some common examples of safety devices and the context in which they can be used:

Trigger lock: A trigger lock is a "shoe" that clamps around the trigger and the trigger guard, preventing the trigger from being operated (**figure 1.10A**, **B**). A key is often used to remove the lock, though sometimes they feature a combination lock. Since a trigger lock has to be installed over the trigger (**figure 1.10B**), you should not use one on a loaded gun, since you could accidentally press the trigger in the process of installing it. Many new handguns come with a trigger lock provided by the manufacturer. If you plan to use your handgun for home defense, a trigger lock may not be the best choice, since you should not use one on a loaded gun. Furthermore, finding the key and unlocking it in a dire situation might prove difficult, especially at night. If you did want to use a trigger lock for a home defense gun, it is imperative that you practice unlocking it, both in the daytime and at night, until you are extremely comfortable with it.

FIGURE 1.10. There are a number of inexpensive options to store your handgun in an inoperable state. **A.** Pictured is an array of different trigger locks. With the turn of the key, the lock comes into two pieces, which can then be reassembled around the trigger guard of the handgun. A dime is included in the picture for size reference. **B.** When installed, a trigger lock prevents the trigger from being accessible. The pictured Glock handgun has a trigger lock installed. **C.** Cable locks can be used to prevent a handgun's slide from properly closing. Pictured are two examples of cable locks.

Cable lock: A cable lock is much like any standard keyed or combination lock, though the locking bar/shackle is replaced with a cable (**figure 1.10C**). With a semiautomatic pistol, the cable prevents a magazine from being inserted and the slide from closing. Most cable locks can be acquired inexpensively, and some manufacturers have started including them with all their handguns.

Gun cases: There are many different cases for storing handguns and long guns, coming in a wide variety of materials, including hard plastic (**figure 1.11A, B**), aluminum, and padded fabric (**figure 1.11C, D**). They are best suited for transporting firearms to and from the shooting range, as opposed to secure, long-term storage. The padding in the cases holds moisture and can contribute to firearms starting to rust if they are stored in the cases. A lock can be added to most cases to prevent a child from accessing the firearm. However, a locked gun case would not prevent a thief from stealing the whole case, and depending on the materials of the case, it could be easily compromised.

FIGURE 1.11. Gun cases are a great way to transport firearms and are available in many different formats. **A.** Many gun cases come in hard plastic, with soft foam inserts (**B**) to protect the handgun from jostling around during transport. **C.** Padded fabric is another popular choice for transporting a handgun or for temporary storage. **D.** The pictured padded fabric case was opened with a simple zipper.

Gun cabinet: A gun cabinet is a more permanent storage solution for your firearms, often coming in the form of a thin-walled steel enclosure with storage racks. Since these cabinets are larger than a gun case, they afford more space to store guns and often have modular shelves and racks depending on whether you plan on storing long guns or handguns. They are not so heavy as to be unmovable by a pair of individuals, at least when they are empty, so they can be moved up and down flights of stairs. Aside from simply offering a place to store your guns, gun cabinets have locking mechanisms so you can keep your firearms secure. These locking mechanisms are not as robust as those found on a gun safe, meaning that forced entry is possible.

Gun safe: The most secure way to store your firearms is in a gun safe (**figure 1.12A, B**). They are made of thicker steel than a gun cabinet and are not easily moved, even when empty. Many gun safes have fireproofing and water resistance, features that most gun cabinets do not offer. The locking mechanisms found on gun safes are often considerably more complex than those found on a gun cabinet, and cannot be forced open. This also means that opening a gun safe is more complicated than opening other storage options, making it a poor choice for storing a home defense gun. With these complicated locking methods, particularly with coded locks, it is essential that you practice opening them.

FIGURE 1.12. A gun safe is the most secure way to store your firearms. **A.** The pictured gun safe uses an electromagnetic-pulse-resistant digital lock and a total of eight locking bolts in the door to prevent the safe from being forced open. **B.** Inside, most gun safes have racks for propping up long guns and shelves for handguns.

A   **B**

Lock boxes / strong boxes: Lock boxes are designed to provide the security of a stationary gun safe, but the portability of a gun case. These containers are made of thick steel but are small enough to be portable. They cannot be easily forced open, but a thief could steal the entire box. Some lock boxes are opened with biometric sensors, recognizing fingerprints. This makes them a reasonable solution for storing a home defense gun, since they can be easily opened even in low-light conditions. If you plan to use a lock box for your home defense handgun storage, you should still practice retrieving it.

1.5. Gun Safety and Children

It is important to talk to your children about the dangers associated with firearms. Depending on the age of the child, they might not fully comprehend the magnitude of what firearms can do and their capacity to cause extreme harm. Firearms are not toys and need to be taken extremely seriously. They are not something to fool around with while trying emulate what you might have seen on television. Even if your firearms are stored safely, you need to prepare for the possibility that one of your children will happen upon a firearm. They could find a firearm in the home of a friend, or a relative, or even in a public place.

1.5.1. Ten Years or Older

Children ten years or older are old enough to understand the safety rules discussed in this chapter, and they should be told to them. If they are interested in shooting, you should consider taking them to the shooting range and guiding them through shooting. This will help demystify firearms and prevent your children from being compelled to seek them out and handle them without proper supervision. When introducing a young person to shooting, it is best to use a small-caliber cartridge such as a .22 Long Rifle (the term "caliber" refers to the diameter of the bullet, measured in inches in this example). The .22 Long Rifle is a good choice because it does not exhibit very much recoil when fired (the recoil is the "kick" that goes along with firing a cartridge), making it very pleasant to shoot, even for those who are not accustomed to shooting. This low recoil is a consequence of the small bullet and the relatively small amount of gunpowder in the cartridge.

1.5.2. Younger than Ten Years Old

If your children are younger than ten years old, you should still stress the dangers that firearms pose, but delving into the details of how to safely handle a firearm is too much for them. Instead, you should tell them that if they come in contact with a firearm, they should not pick it up. Instead, they should inform a responsible adult about the matter, so the adult can deal with it safely. It is important that they do not pick up or handle the firearm. Picking it up greatly increases the chances of someone getting hurt.

1.6. Wear Hearing and Eye Protection While Shooting

The sound of shooting a firearm is extremely loud and can permanently damage your hearing after just a single shot if you are not wearing the proper hearing protection. Noise levels are often measured in decibels (dB), which are a measure of sound pressure. Prolonged exposure to noises at 85 dB can damage your hearing, whereas any noise at 140 dB can potentially permanently damage your hearing with a single exposure. As a point of reference, a conversation at a normal volume level is around 60 dB, whereas the sound of an airplane taking off is somewhere around 140 dB (**table 1.1**). Even a fairly small round such as a .22 Long Rifle creates about 140 dB of noise, whereas more-powerful rifles and handguns are even louder. When firing a gun indoors, the sound can reverberate and perpetuate hearing damage. Because of this, it is important that you wear hearing protection whenever you shoot, even if it is just disposable ear plugs (**figure 1.13A**). Disposable ear plugs are usually made out of a soft foam that you roll up with your fingers and insert into your ears. The foam expands to fit the contours of your ear canal (**figure 1.13B**). For particularly loud firearms, sometimes people will couple disposable ear plugs with ear muffs (**figure 1.13C**). Ear muffs enclose your entire ear (**figure 1.13D**), leaving the ear canal open to insert disposable foam plugs for extra protection.

Individuals who shoot firearms without hearing protection often develop tinnitus, a type of noise-induced hearing loss where the afflicted individual hears a constant ringing sound in their ears in the absence of external noise.

Table 1. Noise levels of common environmental occurrences.
The noise levels of some common occurrences are listed in decibels (dB). Since the dB is on a logarithmic scale, the noise of an airplane taking off is many orders of magnitude louder than that of breathing, despite only a 130-unit difference. Information courtesy of the Center for Hearing and Communication (CHC).

DECIBEL (dB)	ACTIVITY
10	Breathing
30	Whisper
50	Rainfall
50	Refrigerator
60	Conversation, normal volume
80	Telephone ringing
110	Shouting into ear
120	Thunder
120	Chainsaw
140	Airplane taking off
163	Rifle
166	Handgun

FIGURE 1.13. Wearing proper hearing protection and eye protection will help ensure that you can enjoy shooting for years. **A.** Disposable hearing protection usually comes in the form of polyurethane foam plugs. Two different variants are pictured, one with a lanyard for keeping them around your neck when they are not in use. A dime is included for scale. **B.** The disposable foam plugs are rolled up and inserted in your ears. The foam then forms to the shape of your ear canal. Additionally, protective eyewear should always be worn to protect your eyes from ejected cases or flying debris. **C.** Ear muffs are more cumbersome than ear plugs but often offer better protection. **D.** When worn, the ear muffs enclose the entire ear.

ASIDE: WEARING HEARING PROTECTION WHILE HUNTING

Many individuals who hunt do not wear hearing protection while out in the field, because it limits their ability to fully perceive their surroundings. They want to be able to hear the soft crunch of leaves or branches and fear that hearing protection would limit that. Furthermore, most hunters will tell you that in the excitement of staring down a deer, they never actually hear the sound of their gun when they fire it. This is a phenomenon known as auditory exclusion. In situations of high stress or tension, your brain undergoes some physiological adjustments to help you focus on the task at hand and limit other distracting inputs. You lose your peripheral vision and your hearing drops out, allowing you to focus entirely on the deer in front of you. It is important to remember that auditory exclusion is something performed by the brain. Your brain is deciding which inputs to pay attention to and which to ignore. All those inputs are still being collected. Your ears are still picking up on the deafening roar of your rifle, but your brain is not choosing to process the information. So even if you do not notice the sound of your rifle, your ears are still picking it up and your hearing is being damaged.

Since a firearm is loud enough to damage your hearing with just a single shot, you should consider wearing hearing protection while hunting. One solution is to use digital hearing protection, which utilizes microphones to amplify low-level sounds like talking while dampening louder sounds like gunfire. Additionally, if you do not want to pay the increased prices for digital hearing protection, cheaper disposable ear protection can be used, which you put in only when needed. Banded earplugs (**figure 1.14A**) are available that you can have around your neck (**figure 1.14B**) and can easily get into your ears (**figure 1.14C**) without fumbling through your pockets. Since the band keeps both plugs together and in the approximate position they need to be in when wearing them, it is easy to get them in your ears quickly, even when one of your hands is occupied.

FIGURE 1.14. Banded earplugs are a good choice for hunting, since they can be around your neck and easily be put into your ears with one hand. **A.** Banded earplugs consist of soft foam plugs held together by a plastic band. **B.** While hunting, you can have the banded ear plugs around your neck. **C.** When you need to shoot, the band keeps both plugs together, so you do not have to struggle with each individual plug as you try to put them on.

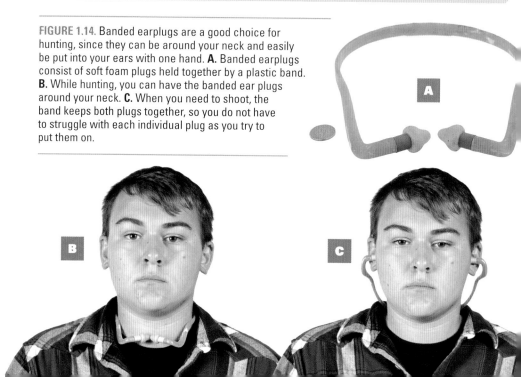

Aside from wearing hearing protection, it is also important that you wear protective eyewear while shooting (**figure 1.13B**, **D**). There is a chance that a bullet will ricochet back at you or that a brass case from an ejected cartridge will catch you in the eye. If you wear prescription glasses, they offer some protection, but not from the sides. So, even if you are wearing glasses, it is advisable to wear proper safety glasses since they offer more complete protection. Just like with your hearing, once you lose your vision, you cannot get it back.

1.7. Never Drink Alcohol While Shooting

Drinking alcohol or taking psychoactive drugs can lead to impaired judgment and decreased coordination, both of which prevent you from using a firearm safely. Because of this, you should never handle firearms under the influence of drugs or alcohol (**figure 1.15**). You should be aware of the side effects of any medication that you are taking, since they could inhibit your ability to safely handle a firearm. If your medication suggests that you should not operate heavy machinery while taking it, then you should not be shooting a handgun while under its influence.

FIGURE 1.15. You should never handle a firearm while under the influence of alcohol or other psychoactive drugs.

224-109783 BG

ANATOMY OF A HANDGUN AND HOW IT WORKS

CHAPTER 2 ANATOMY OF A HANDGUN AND HOW IT WORKS

Most people have a general sense of what a firearm entails, since they all share a number of fundamental design features. In the simplest sense, a firearm is a barrel, essentially a hollow cylinder, from which a projectile is launched. Some form of propellant, customarily gunpowder, is needed to launch the projectile (the bullet) out of the barrel. The gunpowder is rapidly burned, and the pressure built up from the released gas propels the bullet out of the open end of the barrel (the muzzle). In order for sufficient pressure to build up, one end of the barrel needs to be sealed, and the bullet must be tightly seated into the barrel. When the gunpowder is ignited, the only way for the expanding gases to escape is by forcing the bullet out of the barrel.

Older-style muzzle-loading firearms are, as the name implies, loaded from the muzzle end. Gunpowder is poured into the barrel and then a ramrod is used to push a small patch into the barrel to hold the powder in place. The projectile is loaded in last, using the ramrod to push it firmly to the base of the barrel with the powder and patch. The powder is ignited with the help of a piece of flint on the hammer of the firearm (**figure 2.1A, B**). When the flint strikes steel, the resulting sparks are directed into a flash pan / priming pan with a small amount of priming powder (**figure 2.1C**). The sparks ignite the priming powder, which, in turn, ignites the powder behind the bullet through a small hole in the barrel. The design is slow and cumbersome and is particularly problematic in damp weather. The flint and powder pan were later replaced, with the development of the percussion cap (**figure 2.1D**). These small metal caps are filled with a pressure-sensitive explosive that the user places over the top of a metal nipple that provides entry into the barrel (**figure 2.1E**). Once the hammer strikes the percussion cap, it detonates and sends flame through the nipple and into the barrel, igniting the powder and firing the weapon.

The development of the percussion cap led the way to the creation of the metallic cartridge. Rather than loading the gunpowder and the projectile separately into the barrel of the firearm, the metallic cartridge combines them into a single unit (**figure 2.2A**). Specifically, a cartridge consists of the gunpowder and the bullet seated into a metallic case, with a pressure-sensitive unit (a primer) at the base. The primer functions much in the same way as a percussion cap; when the primer is struck, the compound inside burns rapidly and the released gas ignites the rest of the gunpowder in the cartridge (**figure 2.2B**). Gases released from the burning powder build up inside the case, creating a substantial amount of pressure that forces the bullet from the case and down the bore of the barrel (the bore is the hollow portion of the barrel). Since everything is contained in a single, closed unit, the cartridge is not as susceptible to dampness as old muzzle-loading firearms. A cartridge is often mistakenly referred to as a "bullet," though the bullet is just the projectile that actually leaves the barrel of the gun.

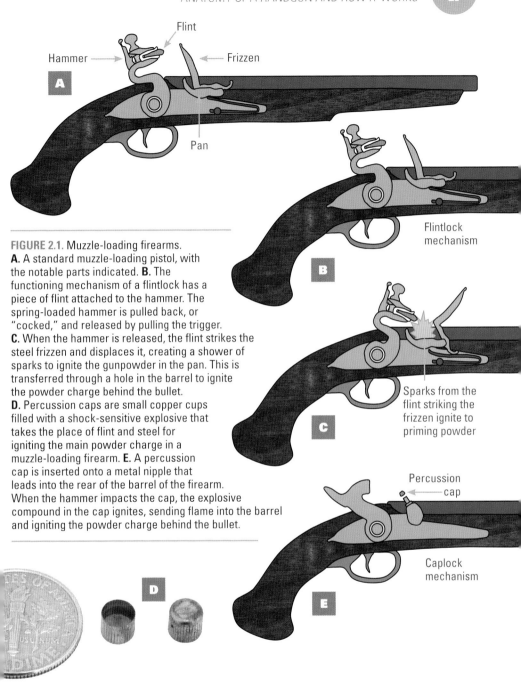

FIGURE 2.1. Muzzle-loading firearms.
A. A standard muzzle-loading pistol, with the notable parts indicated. **B.** The functioning mechanism of a flintlock has a piece of flint attached to the hammer. The spring-loaded hammer is pulled back, or "cocked," and released by pulling the trigger.
C. When the hammer is released, the flint strikes the steel frizzen and displaces it, creating a shower of sparks to ignite the gunpowder in the pan. This is transferred through a hole in the barrel to ignite the powder charge behind the bullet.
D. Percussion caps are small copper cups filled with a shock-sensitive explosive that takes the place of flint and steel for igniting the main powder charge in a muzzle-loading firearm. **E.** A percussion cap is inserted onto a metal nipple that leads into the rear of the barrel of the firearm. When the hammer impacts the cap, the explosive compound in the cap ignites, sending flame into the barrel and igniting the powder charge behind the bullet.

Unlike muzzleloaders, firearms utilizing metallic cartridges are loaded from the rear of the barrel, the breech. These breech-loading firearms need a mechanism for opening the breech to insert a cartridge, and for closing the breech to prevent the escape of gas when the gun is fired. The mechanism that allows for this is referred to as the "action." In a general sense, the action is a collection of parts that determine how the firearm operates, including

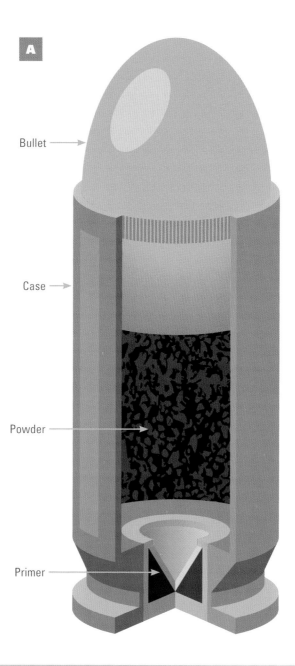

Bullet

Case

Powder

Primer

FIGURE 2.2. The metallic cartridge is a single unit containing the projectile and the gunpowder. **A.** A cutaway image of a metallic cartridge. The projectile (bullet) is fitted into a brass case that stores the gunpowder. A primer at the base of the cartridge is used to ignite the gunpowder to fire the cartridge. **B.** A graphical representation of firing a cartridge, broken down into stages: (1) The cartridge is seated into the chamber. (2) When the trigger is pressed, the firing pin strikes the primer of the cartridge. (3) The impact on the primer ignites the compound inside it, releasing hot gas to ignite the gunpowder in the case. (4) The buildup of gas pressure from the burning powder propels the bullet out of the case and down the barrel. (5) The spiral grooves cut into the barrel impart spin on the bullet, such that it flies in a straight path once leaving the barrel of the gun.

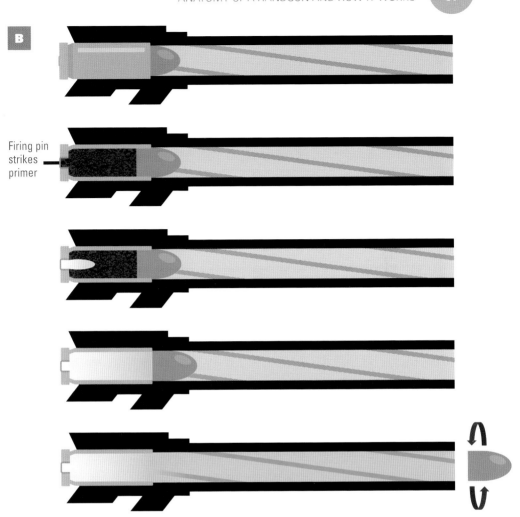

the hammer/striker (for impacting the primer to ignite the gunpowder), the trigger, any safety mechanisms, and, as mentioned above, means to open and close the breech. A plethora of different breech-loading handgun designs exist, broadly falling into two categories: revolvers (**figure 2.3A, B**) and semiautomatic pistols (**figure 2.3C, D**), which will be detailed in sections 2.2 and 2.3, respectively.

2.1. Pistol Components

Handguns come in a wide range of styles, but they all share a number of design features: a barrel, a trigger mechanism, a hammer/striker, an action type for opening and closing the breech, sights, and a frame to hold everything together. Additionally, they have a chamber for holding a cartridge in the ready position for discharge.

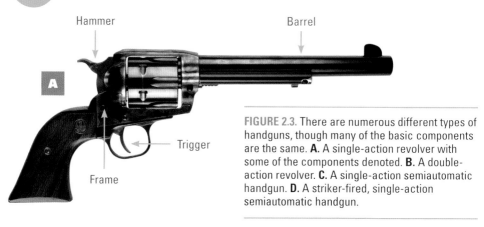

Hammer   Barrel

A

Trigger

Frame

FIGURE 2.3. There are numerous different types of handguns, though many of the basic components are the same. **A.** A single-action revolver with some of the components denoted. **B.** A double-action revolver. **C.** A single-action semiautomatic handgun. **D.** A striker-fired, single-action semiautomatic handgun.

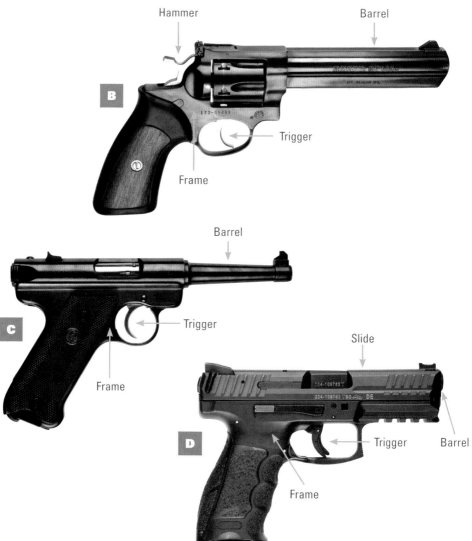

Hammer   Barrel

B

Trigger

Frame

Barrel

C

Trigger

Frame

Slide

D

Trigger

Barrel

Frame

Barrel

One of the most recognizable aspects of the firearm is the barrel, which is simply a metal tube from which the bullet is launched. The hollow portion inside the barrel is referred to as the bore. In older, muzzle-loading firearms, the bore was completely smooth, leading to poor accuracy, since there was nothing to stabilize the round as it left the barrel. Modern firearms have spiral grooves (rifling) cut into the bore, which apply spin to the bullet as it travels down the length of the barrel (**figure 2.4A**). This spin provides stability to the bullet, such that when it leaves the barrel, it stays on target. Cutting grooves into the barrel leaves behind raised areas called "lands" (**figure 2.4B**).The sharp edges of the grooves provide space for the buildup of lead and gunpowder residue from shooting, which can affect accuracy. An increasing number of firearm manufacturers are utilizing polygonal rifling in their handguns, in which a rounded hexagonal or octagonal pattern takes the place of the grooves and lands in standard rifling (**figure 2.4B**). This allows for a tighter seal between the bullet and the bore, allowing for increased gas pressure and yielding higher velocities.

Chamber

At the breech end of the barrel, the bore widens into the chamber, which holds a cartridge in the ready position for firing (**figure 2.4A**). Revolvers do not have the chamber attached to the rear of the barrel. Instead, they have a rotating "cylinder" of separate chambers, one of which locks into place behind the barrel for firing. It is common to hear someone say that they are "chambering" a round, meaning that they are inserting a cartridge into the chamber, making the firearm ready to fire. This can be done manually or through a mechanism on the firearm (which will vary on the basis of the type of handgun).

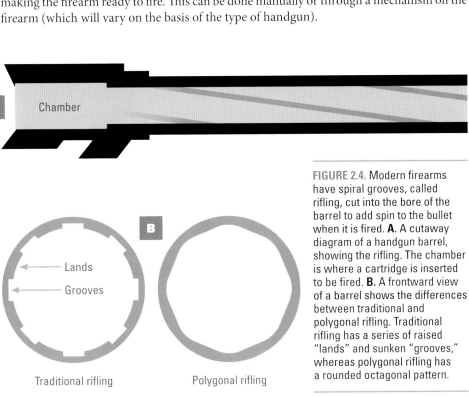

FIGURE 2.4. Modern firearms have spiral grooves, called rifling, cut into the bore of the barrel to add spin to the bullet when it is fired. **A.** A cutaway diagram of a handgun barrel, showing the rifling. The chamber is where a cartridge is inserted to be fired. **B.** A frontward view of a barrel shows the differences between traditional and polygonal rifling. Traditional rifling has a series of raised "lands" and sunken "grooves," whereas polygonal rifling has a rounded octagonal pattern.

Trigger mechanism

The trigger is the part of the firearm that you press to fire it. The trigger does not complete this task in isolation, however; it is part of a collection of components called the trigger mechanism, or trigger group, which work in concert to fire the weapon.

Pressing the trigger releases a striking device that impacts the primer of a cartridge and fires it. There are two primary striking devices: hammers and strikers.

Hammer/striker

The hammer gets its name from its resemblance to the tool both in form and function. It is spring-loaded, and when pulled back on a pivot, or "cocked," tension is put on the spring. This built-up potential energy is converted to kinetic energy when the trigger is pulled, releasing the tension and the hammer. The hammer then strikes the firing pin, which in turn strikes the primer of a cartridge and fires it. A striker has the same end goal as a hammer, but it is essentially just a spring-loaded firing pin. Pulling the trigger will initially push the firing pin backwards and put tension on the spring. Eventually during the backwards arc of the trigger, the spring will be released and the firing pin will be propelled forward, striking the cartridge and firing it. There is no hammer to hit the firing pin into the cartridge; the firing pin itself is propelled into the cartridge when the spring tension is released.

Action

Action is a general term that includes all the mechanisms in place for a firearm to function. The action needs to be able to open the breech, insert a cartridge, and then seal the breech to prevent pressurized gas from escaping when the gun is fired. The aforementioned trigger mechanism and hammer/striker help make up the action of a handgun.

Most semiautomatic handguns have what is known as a slide that moves backwards and forwards during the operating cycle of the gun. The slide usually holds the firing pin or the striker, and the extractor. In its forward position, the slide seals the rear opening of the barrel (the breech) to prevent pressurized gas from escaping when a cartridge is fired. The slide is propelled backwards once a cartridge is fired. During this backwards motion, the extractor removes the empty case and ejects it from the chamber. This backwards movement puts pressure on a recoil spring in the slide. When the slide reaches its rearmost position, the compressed recoil spring pushes the slide forward. The forward motion picks up a new cartridge from the magazine and inserts it into the chamber, readying the gun to fire another round.

Some other breech-loading firearms have what is known as a bolt to prevent pressurized gas from escaping from the breech when a cartridge is fired. Similar to a slide, the bolt then moves backwards to remove the spent case, and then moves forward to load a new cartridge from the magazine. Oftentimes, the firing pin and extractor are components of the bolt. Bolts are not as common in handguns as they are in rifles, but they are found in the Ruger Standard Model/MK II/MK III/MK IV pistol, one of the most popular pistols that fires .22 Long Rifle cartridges.

Action classification is partially determined by how many functions the firearm's trigger performs. A "single-action" handgun requires that you manually pull back the hammer. A part of the trigger mechanism, called the sear, keeps the hammer in the cocked position until the trigger is pressed, which releases the hammer, firing the handgun. The trigger performs only a "single" action: releasing the hammer/striker. Many older-style revolvers are single-action (described further in section 2.2). With a "double-action" handgun, the trigger has two jobs: setting the hammer and then releasing it to fire the weapon.

Sights

Every handgun has a set of alignment markers built into the barrel, or the slide, to help with aiming the firearm, called iron sights. These sights consist of two components, a front sight and a rear sight. There are many different sight permutations, but the most common has a single post at the front of the barrel (**figure 2.5A**) and a notched sight at the rear of the barrel (**figure 2.5B**). These two sights need to be aligned on the target if you want to hit it accurately (**figure 2.5C**).

Frame

The frame is what holds all the working parts of the handgun together. It collects the trigger mechanism, the barrel, and all the components needed for loading a cartridge into the chamber and sealing it. The handle of the handgun is also part of the frame. The frame is what is legally considered the firearm as per United States law and must contain a serial number for identification purposes, according to the Gun Control Act of 1968.

Traditionally, frames were made of steel, though polymer frames have become increasingly more popular with the success of Glock pistols, due to their lightness and durability. With rifles, the frame is often called a receiver, but it fulfills all the same roles.

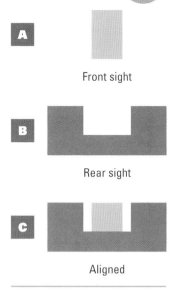

FIGURE 2.5. Handguns have a set of alignment markers for aiming, called iron sights. **A.** The front sight on a handgun is almost universally some form of a straight post. **B.** The rear sight is most commonly notched. **C.** The front sight is aligned between the two sides of the notched rear sight.

Safety mechanisms

Any firearm built today has mechanisms built into it called safeties, which prevent the firearm from being fired accidentally. These safeties can be divided into two main types: active safeties and passive safeties. When most people think of a safety on a firearm, they are thinking of active safeties (sometimes called manual safeties). These come in the form of a lever or a button that can manually be set to a "safe" position to impede the firearm from discharging. These safeties come in many different forms but generally function by preventing the trigger from moving (**figure 2.6A**), or by disengaging the trigger from the firing mechanism. Additionally, some prevent the slide from moving and disengage the sear from the hammer (**figure 2.6B**).

Passive safeties are those that the user does not need to activate; they function automatically. This includes such mechanisms as drop safeties, grip safeties, and trigger safeties. As the name suggests, a drop safety prevents the handgun from discharging if it is dropped. It does this by preventing the firing mechanism from functioning unless the trigger is depressed. A grip safety is a lever built into the handle that needs to be fully depressed for the handgun to be fired (**figure 2.6C**). These safeties make sure that the user is properly holding the handgun before it can be discharged, so it cannot be fired before the user is ready. Trigger safeties prevent the handgun from firing unless the trigger is intentionally depressed. In this case, the trigger consists of two separate parts, both of which need to be fully depressed to fire the handgun. This often takes the form of a "trigger within a trigger," with one smaller trigger extending beyond the primary trigger (**figure 2.6D**). If your finger accidentally flicks part of the trigger,

A Active safety

B Active safety

C Grip safety

D Trigger safety

FIGURE 2.6. Handgun safeties come in multiple forms, from active safeties that the user must set, to passive safeties that function automatically. **A.** An active safety on a Smith & Wesson Shield, which prevents the trigger from moving when slid upward. The safety is engaged in the picture. **B.** An active safety of a Les Baer 1911 pistol, which prevents the slide from moving and disengages the sear from the hammer. The safety is engaged in the picture. **C.** A passive grip safety on a Les Baer 1911 pistol. The pistol will fire only if the grip safety is fully depressed, which can be accomplished by gripping it properly. **D.** A passive trigger safety on a Glock 19 pistol. The trigger consists of two separate parts, each of which needs to be fully depressed to fire the handgun.

it will not set off the gun, since both parts need to be fully depressed. This type of safety was popularized by Glock pistols, but now it is found on many polymer-framed handguns.

It cannot be stressed enough that the user is the primary factor that determines whether the firearm is safe. The passive safeties on firearms are to prevent accidental discharge. They cannot prevent careless gun handling. Having an active safety on your handgun is of little consequence if you do not follow the three rules of safe gun handling (section 1.1). Just because you have the active safety engaged on your handgun does not make it safe to point the gun at someone or yourself.

2.2. Revolvers

Revolvers are one of the oldest types of modern handguns. Their name is derived from the action mechanism that they employ, using a rotating cylinder with multiple chambers, usually five or six. When they were first designed, loading a handgun was a lengthy process, since the metallic cartridge had not been developed yet, so anything that could fire multiple shots before reloading was a tremendous boon. Flintlock revolvers started to see use in the early 1800s, before being replaced by percussion cap revolvers. The first patented percussion cap revolver was designed by Samuel Colt in the mid-1830s, ushering in widespread usage of the revolver design. The 1850s saw the introduction of the first revolver using metallic cartridges, and the design has been popular ever since.

Revolvers generally fall into two categories, based on the action mechanism they use: single-action or double-action.

Single-action

The first revolvers were all single-action, and the majority of single-action revolvers today are replicas of old designs. If you can imagine the sort of firearms used in a Clint Eastwood western film, you have a good idea of what a single-action revolver looks like (**figure 2.7A**).

The trigger of a single-action revolver performs only one action; it releases the hammer to fire the gun. When the revolver's hammer is pulled back, the cylinder rotates to align a new chamber with the barrel of the gun. Pressing the trigger releases the hammer to fire the gun. Cocking the hammer again will rotate the just-fired chamber away from the

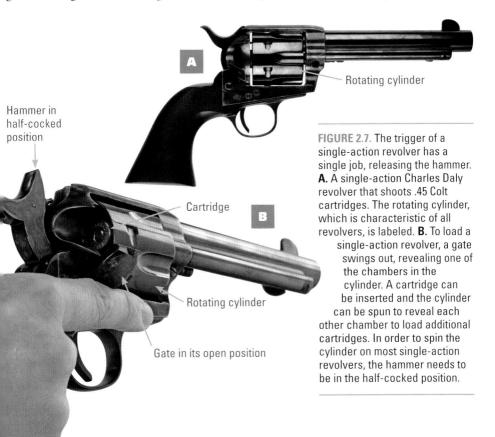

Hammer in half-cocked position

Rotating cylinder

Cartridge

Rotating cylinder

Gate in its open position

FIGURE 2.7. The trigger of a single-action revolver has a single job, releasing the hammer. **A.** A single-action Charles Daly revolver that shoots .45 Colt cartridges. The rotating cylinder, which is characteristic of all revolvers, is labeled. **B.** To load a single-action revolver, a gate swings out, revealing one of the chambers in the cylinder. A cartridge can be inserted and the cylinder can be spun to reveal each other chamber to load additional cartridges. In order to spin the cylinder on most single-action revolvers, the hammer needs to be in the half-cocked position.

barrel and align a new chamber with the barrel, readying it for firing. The user must manually set the hammer by pulling it back. All the earliest revolver designs were single-action.

The majority of single-action revolvers are loaded through a gate at the side of the handgun, which exposes a single chamber (**figure 2.7B**). Once a cartridge is inserted into the empty chamber, the cylinder can be rotated to load the other chambers. In order to rotate the cylinder to load rounds, many revolvers require that the hammer is in a half-cocked position. After all the cartridges are fired, each case must be individually ejected through the loading gate, with the help of an ejector rod.

Double-action

A double-action revolver (**figure 2.8A**) does not require that the user manually set the hammer. Pressing the trigger does two things in succession: it sets the hammer, and then it releases the hammer. By virtue of having to perform both these functions, there is a much more substantial "trigger pull" (trigger pull is a general term referring to the amount of force that you need to apply to a trigger before it releases the hammer to fire the weapon). A double-action trigger has a substantially longer travel time than a single-action trigger, along with more resistance.

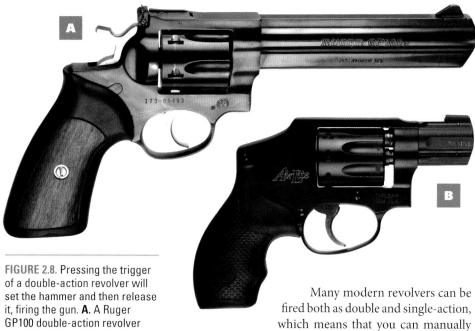

FIGURE 2.8. Pressing the trigger of a double-action revolver will set the hammer and then release it, firing the gun. **A.** A Ruger GP100 double-action revolver that shoots .357 Magnum cartridges. The revolver can be fired single-action if the user manually pulls back the hammer. **B.** A Smith & Wesson AirLite double-action revolver that shoots .22 Long Rifle cartridges. It can only be fired double-action because the hammer is not exposed and cannot be manually set.

Many modern revolvers can be fired both as double and single-action, which means that you can manually set the hammer and shoot it as a single-action, or you can let the trigger set the hammer, and shoot it as a double-action. When shooting it single-action, the distance the trigger has to travel when pressing it is much shorter, since you have already performed one of its jobs. If you do not manually set the trigger, the distance the trigger has to travel is longer, since it first has to set the trigger and then release it.

There are some revolvers that can be fired only double-action (**figure 2.8B**). Most of these are designed

FIGURE 2.9. The cylinders of most double-action revolvers swing out of the frame, allowing each chamber to be loaded easily. **A.** A Smith & Wesson Model 10 double-action revolver with the cylinder in its open position. A single dummy round is in one of the chambers, while the others are empty. **B.** Pressing the extractor rod pushes the extractor out of the cylinder, pulling the cartridges partially out of the cylinder for easy removal.

ASIDE: AVOID SNAPPING THE CYLINDER OPEN AND CLOSED.

Since the cylinder on a double-action revolver can swing outward, you might have the urge to snap it open with a satisfying flip of the wrist or deftly snap it shut after inserting new cartridges. This is not advised, since it can bend the piece that holds the cylinder to the frame, the crane. Any feeling of satisfaction you have after performing the action will dissolve when you realize you have damaged your handgun.

as self-defense revolvers, where the hammer is shrouded and not exposed. This means that you cannot manually pull back the hammer, making it impossible to shoot it single-action. The shrouded hammer prevents it from snagging on clothing when you go to draw it from a holster, making it well-suited for concealed carry. The more substantial trigger pull helps ensure that in a defensive situation, under high levels of stress, you do not unintentionally fire the gun.

Loading and unloading a double-action revolver is easier and more expedient than a single-action revolver. The cylinder in a double-action revolver swings out of the frame, exposing all the chambers at once (**figure 2.9A**). This allows new cartridges to be loaded concurrently. By pressing the ejector rod that is concentrically attached to the cylinder, the ejector rises out of the cylinder and pulls the cartridges out with it (**figure 2.9B**).

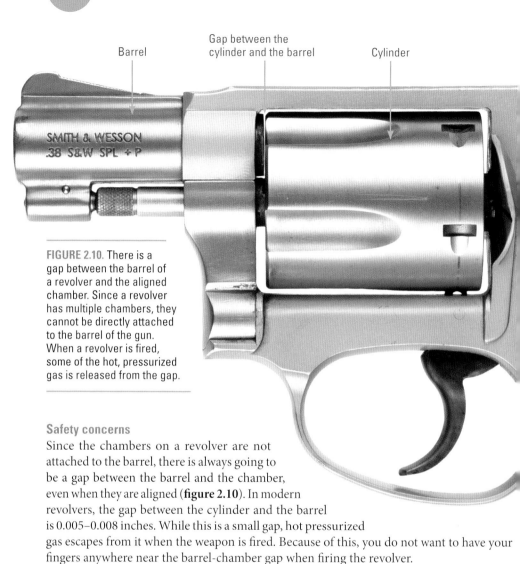

Barrel

Gap between the cylinder and the barrel

Cylinder

SMITH & WESSON
.38 S&W SPL + P

FIGURE 2.10. There is a gap between the barrel of a revolver and the aligned chamber. Since a revolver has multiple chambers, they cannot be directly attached to the barrel of the gun. When a revolver is fired, some of the hot, pressurized gas is released from the gap.

Safety concerns

Since the chambers on a revolver are not attached to the barrel, there is always going to be a gap between the barrel and the chamber, even when they are aligned (**figure 2.10**). In modern revolvers, the gap between the cylinder and the barrel is 0.005–0.008 inches. While this is a small gap, hot pressurized gas escapes from it when the weapon is fired. Because of this, you do not want to have your fingers anywhere near the barrel-chamber gap when firing the revolver.

Unlike semiautomatic handguns, very few revolvers have manually activated safety mechanisms. With a single-action revolver, since you have to actively set the hammer before pulling the trigger will fire it, the likelihood of someone unintentionally doing both of these things by accident is low. The considerable trigger pull on a double-action revolver helps ensure that you are not fully pressing the trigger unless that is your intention.

2.3. Semiautomatic Pistols

Semiautomatic handguns came into being when designers realized that they could harness the energy of a recoiling handgun and use it to do work; namely, ejecting the empty case and loading a new round into the chamber. A semiautomatic handgun will fire a cartridge every time that you pull the trigger of the gun, the energy of the discharged round cycling the action of the firearm and loading a new cartridge. This process involves ejecting the case of the spent cartridge, recocking the hammer/striker, and then inserting a new cartridge into the chamber, generally feeding it from a detachable magazine. A fully automatic firearm does all the same things but will continue to fire additional cartridges if the trigger remains depressed. A semiautomatic will fire only a single round with a single press of the trigger; it will not fire another round until the trigger resets and is repressed.

ASIDE: MAGAZINE VS. CLIP

When referring to the detachable cartridge holder in a handgun, the terms "magazine" and "clip" are often used interchangeably, but they are technically not the same.

A magazine stores cartridges and feeds them into position to be picked up by the gun's action and loaded into the chamber (**figure 2.11A**). Magazines are usually detachable and are spring-loaded to push a new round into position after one is fired and the empty case is ejected. A magazine functions much like a PEZ dispenser. After a piece of PEZ candy is removed from the dispenser, a new piece is pushed up to take the place of the removed piece.

A clip is considerably less complicated than a magazine. It keeps multiple rounds together in a unit, such that they can be easily and efficiently pushed into a magazine of a firearm (**figure 2.11B**). Usually they are used to put cartridges into a firearm that has a magazine that is not removable (**figure 2.12A, B**). You push the cartridges out of the clip and into the magazine and remove the empty clip. The clip is then discarded or, more likely, saved for future use (**figure 2.12C, D**). A clip is usually a small metal unit that holds the cartridges together at their bases. They are most common with older military battle rifles and are often referred to as "stripper clips."

FIGURE 2.11. The terms "magazine" and "clip" are often used interchangeably, but they are not the same thing. **A.** A magazine is an ammunition-feeding device that pushes a new cartridge into position to be loaded into the chamber after a cartridge is fired. Pictured is an empty magazine (*left*) and a loaded magazine (*right*) from a 9 × 19 mm Glock pistol. **B.** A clip keeps multiple cartridges together so they can be pushed into a magazine. Pictured is a partially loaded clip (*left*) and a fully loaded clip (*right*). The clip is holding 9 × 23 mm Steyr cartridges for use in a Steyr M1912 pistol.

FIGURE 2.12. A clip is used to load cartridges into the magazine of a firearm. **A.** Pictured is a Steyr M1912 pistol. It has a spring-loaded magazine in the handle, but it is not removable. **B.** The slide of the Steyr M1912 has been pulled back, allowing the internal magazine to be loaded from above. **C.** A clip holding 9 × 23 mm cartridges is inserted into the pistol, situated above the integral magazine. **D.** By applying force to the cartridges, the cartridges are pushed into the internal magazine and off the clip. The clip can then be removed.

2.3.1. Action Mechanisms

Nearly all semiautomatic handguns have the same basic components (**figure 2.13A, B, C, D**). They have a metal slide that slides backward (**figure 2.13C**) on rails (**figure 2.13D**) on the frame of the gun. The barrel of the gun is either anchored to the frame or separate and housed within the slide. The gun's firing pin is stored within the slide, along with an extractor (**figure 2.13C**) for removing the empty case after the round is fired. Despite having basically the same components, they do not all function identically. The actions of semiautomatic firearms can be grouped into three different categories: (1) blowback operation, (2) recoil operation, and (3) gas operation.

1. Blowback operation

Handguns using the blowback method of operation utilize the energy from the expelled case of a fired round to operate the action. When a round is fired, the buildup of pressurized gases in the case pushes the bullet through the barrel but also pushes the empty case out of the chamber. The case contacts the slide (or, in some cases, the bolt; **figure 2.14A**), pushing it rearward. Only the slide/bolt moves backward; the barrel is often fixed to the frame and remains in place (**figure 2.14B**). The weight of the slide/bolt and the stiffness of the recoil spring impede the slide/bolt movement long enough for the bullet to clear the barrel of the gun. This short delay in slide/bolt movement is essential; otherwise the user will be hit by hot gas erupting from the ejection port on the slide, or the frame (**figure 2.14B**). When the slide/bolt does move backward, the extractor seated into it catches the empty case, ejecting it through the ejection port. Once the slide/bolt reaches its apex, the fully compressed recoil spring drives it forward, chambering a new cartridge as it does so, readying the gun for shooting another round.

    This mechanism is usually used with smaller-caliber cartridges such as .22 Long Rifle and .380 ACP. These cartridges exhibit pressures low enough that a heavy slide/bolt and stiff recoil spring can keep the slide closed long enough for a bullet to clear the barrel. Higher-pressure cartridges would necessitate heavier slides/bolts and recoil springs, stiff enough that pulling back the slide would be challenging.

2. Recoil operation

For handguns shooting more-powerful rounds than .22 Long Rifle, recoil operation is the most common design. With this operating mechanism, the barrel is a separate piece that locks into the slide. When a round is fired, the barrel and slide are propelled backward in unison for a short time, before they separate from one another. The barrel disconnects from the slide shortly after the bullet leaves the barrel of the gun. After the separation, the slide continues backward on its own, compressing the recoil spring and extracting the empty case. The built-up energy in the compressed recoil spring then compels the slide forward, reconnecting with the barrel and loading in a new cartridge from the magazine. Most semiautomatic handguns use recoil operation.

3. Gas operation

While it is somewhat uncommon, gas operation is another mechanism used for semiautomatic handguns. As the name implies, the firearms utilize the highly pressurized gas from a fired cartridge to work the action. Once a cartridge is fired, pressurized gas is diverted through a hole in the barrel. This gas is directed to a piston, driving it backward and working the action of the pistol. This usually entails propelling a slide rearward, ejecting the empty case, and then feeding in a new cartridge, readying it for a new shot.

Chamber

Slide

A

Trigger guard

Frame   Trigger

Slide

Slide stop

B

Magazine release

Extractor   Ejection port   Barrel

C

Slide

Barrel

D

Recoil spring

Rail

Frame

FIGURE 2.13. Most semiautomatic handguns feature many of the same general components. **A.** The left side of a Glock 19 semiautomatic handgun, with some of the common features labeled. While the barrel of the gun is largely obscured by the slide, the chamber is visible. **B.** The right side of a Glock 19 semiautomatic handgun, with the slide stop and magazine release clearly visible. **C.** The slide of the Glock 19 has been locked back, revealing the barrel. **D.** A disassembled view of the Glock 19. The rail that the slide moves upon has been labeled.

Bolt

A

FIGURE 2.14. Blowback-operated semiautomatic handguns utilize the rearward motion of the cartridge case to cycle the action. **A.** A blowback-operated handgun chambered in a .22 Long Rifle. In place of a slide, the handgun features a retractable bolt. **B.** The same blowback-operated handgun with its bolt fully retracted. When a cartridge is fired, the pressurized gas that builds up pushes the empty case against the bolt, forcing it back.

Bolt   Ejection port

B

Gas operation is most commonly used in rifles, though a notable handgun example is Israel Weapon Industries / Magnum Research's venerable Desert Eagle pistol. The Desert Eagle was the first handgun designed to shoot the .50 Action Express cartridge, which is one of the largest handgun calibers in the world. The gas operation system allows the larger-caliber rounds, traditionally designated only for magnum revolvers, to be fired in a semiautomatic pistol.

2.3.2. Trigger Mechanisms

As with revolvers, the trigger mechanisms in semiautomatic handguns fall into two main camps (single-action and double-action), though differentiating between the types is not as easy to do visually.

Single-action

For a single-action semiautomatic, the hammer/striker needs to be manually set, usually by pulling back the slide. The sole thing that the trigger does is release the hammer/striker. It needs only to be manually set for the first round, since the reciprocating slide will set the hammer/striker for each subsequent shot. Because of the limited role of the trigger, the trigger pull is usually short and distinct. A good example of a single-action semiautomatic handgun is the Colt M1911, the standard-issue sidearm for the US military from 1911 until 1985.

Double-action

Some semiautomatic handguns can be fired both as double and single-action. These are usually handguns that have a hammer, as opposed to a striker. They have a slide that sets the hammer when it is pulled back, such that the shot will have a light, single-action trigger. Since you need to pull back the slide and release it to feed a cartridge into the chamber, the hammer will be set, and the trigger will be single-action. Where does double-action come into play? Double-action handguns have a decocking device to lower the hammer after it has been set, allowing you to carry the gun with a round in the chamber, but with the hammer down. When you go to shoot the gun, the first trigger pull will be heavy, since it first needs to set the hammer and then release it. The first shot is the only one that will be double-action, since the retracting slide will set the hammer for the second shot. This design can be appealing to people who want to carry a gun for defense but do not feel comfortable carrying it cocked with a light trigger pull (fearing that in the pressure of a defensive situation, they might fire their gun unintentionally). A double-action semiautomatic handgun allows you to carry it with a round in the chamber, ready to fire, but with a substantial double-action trigger pull.

The Beretta M9 is a notable example of a double-action semiautomatic handgun, which served as a sidearm for the US armed forces from 1985 to 2017.

3

AMMUNITION

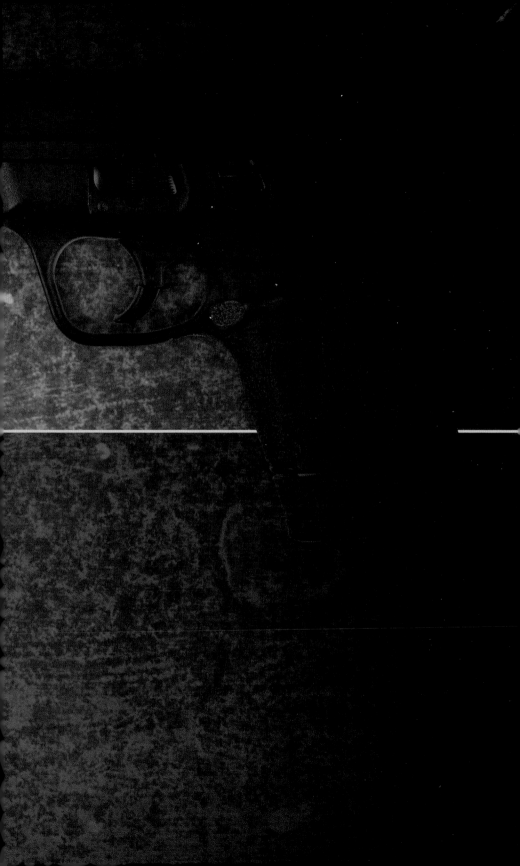

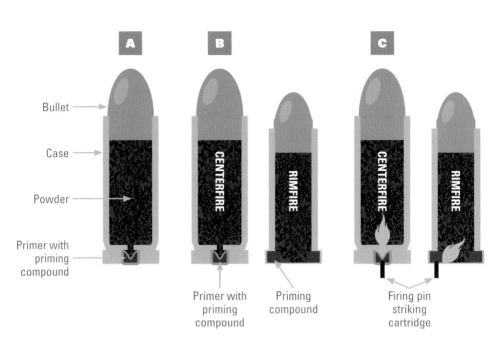

FIGURE 3.1. Modern firearms shoot metallic cartridges, which combine the bullet, gunpowder, a pressure-sensitive priming element, and a case into a single unit. **A.** Pictured is a cutaway image showing the components of a metallic cartridge. **B.** There are two types of metallic cartridges, centerfire and rimfire. Centerfire cartridges have their pressure-sensitive priming compound in a primer that is set into the base of the case. Rimfire cartridges have the priming compound between the folds of the rim of the case. **C.** When a handgun is fired, the firing pin strikes the primer, or the rim of a rimfire cartridge, crushes part of it, and ignites the priming compound. The ignited priming compound then ignites the gunpowder in the case.

All modern firearms shoot metallic cartridges, making shooting them considerably easier than shooting firearms from the era of muzzle loaders. A cartridge, also called a "round," combines all the aspects needed to fire a projectile into a single unit. It contains the projectile (the bullet), the gunpowder, a pressure-sensitive element to ignite the gunpowder (a pressure-sensitive priming compound), and a metal case to hold them all together (**figure 3.1A**). It is very common for people to refer to a cartridge as a "bullet," though that is not technically correct, since the bullet is just one component of the cartridge. There are two main metallic cartridge designs, centerfire and rimfire, which differ in the position of the pressure-sensitive priming compound (**figure 3.1B**). A centerfire cartridge has the priming compound in a primer that is seated into the base of the cartridge, whereas a rimfire cartridge has the priming compound inside a folded crevice in the rim of the case. To ignite the cartridge, the firing pin of the firearm strikes the primer, or the rim of a rimfire cartridge. This impact crushes the priming compound and ignites it, which then ignites the gunpowder in the case (**figure 3.1C**). The hot gases released from the combustion of the powder cause the case to expand inside the chamber, sealing it and allowing enough pressure to build to force the bullet from the case and out of the barrel. After the bullet leaves the barrel, the pressure drops and the case relaxes inside the chamber, allowing it to be easily removed.

Generally, the larger the bullet, the more gunpowder that will be in the cartridge. The increase in the amount of gunpowder used means that higher pressures will be generated when the cartridge is fired. In order for a rimfire cartridge to fire, the walls of the case need to be thin enough to be crushed by the firing pin. However, if there is too much gunpowder and pressures get too high, it could easily rupture the thin walls of the case. Because of this, rimfire is generally reserved for cartridges with smaller bullets and less gunpowder. Currently, the .22 Long Rifle is one of the only rimfire cartridges commonly produced, though it is also one of the most popular cartridges available, since it is relatively inexpensive.

3.1. Components of a Cartridge

The world of firearms is flush with a tremendous number of different cartridge types. This is made possible by variations in every cartridge component: the bullet, the case, the primer/pressure-sensitive element, and the powder. Each of these components will be addressed separately.

3.1.1. Bullet

The bullet is the actual projectile that is fired out of a handgun. The diameter of the bullet is referred to as its "caliber," which is measured in millimeters (mm) or in inches. Bullets come in a variety of configurations depending on their intended use. They are typically made of lead (**figure 3.2A**), though sometimes the lead is surrounded by a thin layer of copper. The copper can be added via two methods: (1) electroplating (**figure 3.2B**), where copper is chemically applied by a process called electrodeposition, or (2) by filling a copper "jacket" with lead (**figure 3.2C**). The copper layer on a jacketed bullet is often thicker than that on an electroplated bullet, though it is often hard to differentiate electroplated bullets from jacketed bullets by eye. Jacketed bullets were necessitated by the push to make bullets for higher-velocity applications, since the pressurized gas from firing a cartridge would begin to melt the surface of the lead bullet as it passed through the barrel. Copper is harder than lead and has a higher melting point,

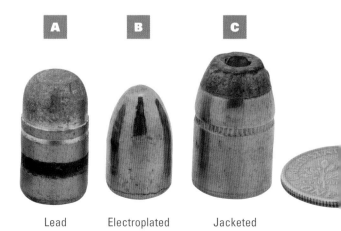

FIGURE 3.2. Virtually all bullets are made of lead (**A**), although some lead bullets are covered by a thin coat of copper. The copper coat is applied by electroplating (**B**), or the lead is poured into a jacket of copper (**C**). A dime is included for scale.

Lead   Electroplated   Jacketed

FIGURE 3.3. Most defensive cartridges have a hollowed-out tip that expands upon impacting the target. These "hollow-point" rounds come in various designs. Cartridge identity (*from left to right*): 9 × 19 mm Parabellum, 9 × 19 mm Parabellum with a plastic plug, .40 S & W, .45 ACP, .45 Colt, .50 Action Express. A dime is included for scale.

allowing the bullet to stay intact as it leaves the barrel. This also helps prevent lead residue from building up in the grooves of the barrel, which can affect accuracy if the firearm is not properly cleaned.

Lead bullets are more economical to shoot than jacketed bullets, but the lead poses a health concern. Lead is toxic to many organs, including the heart, kidneys, intestines, bones, and nervous system, so ingesting it can have serious ramifications for your health. Early stages of lead poisoning are marked by joint and muscle pain, headaches, memory loss, and impaired mental functioning. Shooting in enclosed and poorly ventilated areas can result in the inhalation of lead particulates, and if you do not properly wash your hands after handling lead bullets or spent casings from fired rounds, it can easily be ingested. Aside from health effects, lead residue builds up in the rifling of the barrel (known as lead fouling) and will affect accuracy if not regularly, and properly, cleaned. Lead bullets are generally not pure lead; they are usually an alloy of antimony and other trace metals that increase the bullet's hardness. The lead alloy needs to be soft enough for the bullet's base to expand from the heat of the combustion gases to fill the bore and form a seal, allowing sufficient pressure to build up to launch the bullet. However, if the alloy is too soft, the hot gases will start to melt the bullet and the gas will leak past it, resulting in lead depositing in the bore when the bullet clears the barrel. If the lead alloy is too hard, on the other hand, the base will not properly expand to seal the hot gases behind it. These hot gases will escape around the sides of the bullet, which also results in excessive lead fouling in the barrel. The proper lead hardness for a bullet depends on the cartridge and the velocity that the bullet is supposed to obtain. Higher-velocity bullets achieve that with more gunpowder and more pressurized hot gas, which will melt the lead alloy if it is not of a sufficient hardness. For this reason, most rifle cartridges have jacketed bullets because the amount of pressurized gas required to meet the proper velocities would melt the lead.

Electroplated bullets do not foul the barrel as much, since the metal coating prevents the lead from melting. Additionally, they are not as much of a health concern when they are handled. These benefits come at a higher price point, however. The same benefits of electroplated bullets apply to jacketed bullets. Firing jacketed bullets does not soil the barrel as quickly as lead bullets, but the metal coating does cause more wear on the barrel. However, with modern firearms, it would take well over 100,000 jacketed rounds before the barrel has noticeable wear, which is more than most people will put through a handgun. If you are shooting lead bullets, as opposed to jacketed bullets, you will likely never wear out the barrel of a handgun. It should be noted that with higher-velocity rifle rounds, jacketed bullets can have more of an effect. As an example, many competition shooters who use AR-15s will have their rifle barrels inspected for wear after 10,000 rounds. However, judging the wear of a barrel simply by round count is difficult. If you shoot a few hundred rounds in a few hours, it will overheat the barrel and produce more wear than shooting that same amount over a protracted period of time.

Outside of their composition, bullets can be divided into two categories: defensive and target. As the name suggests, defensive bullets are designed to defend oneself. They generally have the tip hollowed out to create what is known as a "hollow point" (**figure 3.3**) This allows for the bullet to expand upon impact, increasing its diameter and causing additional tissue damage while decreasing the level of penetration.

Target bullets are used for everyday shooting practice, generally do not have hollow points, and are cheaper. Target bullets can come in a wide variety of shapes, including wadcutter (**figure 3.4A**), semiwadcutter (**figure 3.4B**), round-nosed flat-point (**figure 3.4C**), and round nose (**figure 3.4D**), to name just a few.

Wadcutter bullets are specially designed, flat-fronted bullets that do not have a conical tip. The width of the bullet stays the same for its entire length. They were designed for competition shooting, since they punch clean holes in the target, with minimal tearing of the paper, which is common of rounded bullets. However, the flat heads of the bullets often pose problems when being fed from a magazine and are usually reserved for revolvers, unless a particular semiautomatic pistol was specifically designed to shoot them. A semiwadcutter combines aspects of wadcutter and round-nosed bullets to make them easier to feed in semiautomatic pistols. The bullets are conical like a round-nosed bullet, but the tip has a flat point for making clean holes in paper. A round-nosed, flat-point bullet is essentially a round-nosed bullet with the tip cut off, making it flat. This type of bullet is popular with Cowboy Action shooters, since it functions well both in single-action revolvers and lever-action rifles (Cowboy Action shooting is a competitive shooting sport that celebrates the shooting style

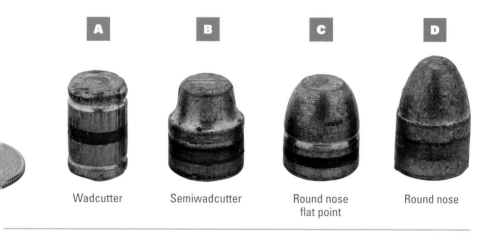

Wadcutter   Semiwadcutter   Round nose   Round nose
                                          flat point

FIGURE 3.4. Bullets for target shooting come in many different shapes. **A.** Wadcutters are designed to punch clean holes in paper targets for competition shooting. **B.** Semiwadcutters maintain some of the flat-tipped profile of a wadcutter but are beveled to help them feed more easily in semiautomatic pistols. **C.** Round-nosed, flat-point bullets are round-nosed bullets with the tip cut off. **D.** Round-nosed bullets are good general-purpose bullets that feed easily from a magazine. A dime is included for scale.

and culture of the American Old West of the late nineteenth century). Round-nosed bullets are smooth and curved, making them ideal for smoothly feeding from a magazine into the chamber, but they do not puncture paper as cleanly on a target.

3.1.2. Case

In simple terms, a case is a hollow tube that has an open end, wherein the bullet is inserted, and a closed end at the base. It holds the bullet in place and aligns it with the bore, along with storing the gunpowder and providing a place for its combustion when the round is fired. There are two main types of cartridges, rimfire and centerfire. The base of a centerfire case has a pocket for holding a primer that contains a pressure-sensitive priming compound (see section 3.1.3). A rimfire case does not have a primer pocket, instead having a folded rim at the base, holding the pressure-sensitive priming compound (see section 3.1.3). When the firing pin strikes the rear of the case, the impact crushes the top and bottom of the rim together, which crushes the priming compound within, igniting it.

The cases are constructed of brass, nickel-plated brass, steel, or aluminum. Many people will collect the empty cases after shooting and reload them (see section 3.5), but this can easily be done only with brass and nickel-plated cases. Most handgun cartridges have cases with a straight body, meaning the case has a consistent diameter for its entire length. More uncommonly, some have a bottleneck shape with a body that is thicker than the mouth, with the two portions meeting with a slanted shoulder. This bottleneck design allows more powder to be used with a smaller bullet. Increasing the amount of powder supplies more gas from combustion, all of which is forced into a smaller mouth, resulting in higher pressures, which launch the bullet at a higher velocity. The bottleneck design is most common with rifle cartridges that are designed to achieve higher velocities.

Another differentiator for case type is the flange at the bottom of the case, which is known as a rim. The extractor of a firearm will hook onto this rim when it is removing a spent case from the chamber once the cartridge has been fired. There are five different case types differing in the diameter of the rim with respect to the diameter of the rest of the case: rimmed, semirimmed, rimless, rebated rim, and belted.

1. Rimmed

As the name suggests, rimmed cases have a rim that extends beyond the body of the case, the rim having a larger diameter than the body (**figure 3.5A**). This type is often used in revolvers where the rim prevents the cartridge from setting too deeply in the chamber, providing what is known as "headspacing" control. Some revolvers can fire a number of

FIGURE 3.5. There is a wide assortment of different case designs.
A. A rimmed .38 Special revolver cartridge. Note how the rim at the bottom of the case extends beyond the body of the case.
B. A semirimmed .32 ACP pistol cartridge. Note that the rim at the bottom of the case extends slightly beyond the body of the case.
C. A rimless 9 × 19 mm Parabellum pistol cartridge. While a rim is present, it does not extend beyond the body of the case.
D. A rebated-rim .50 AE pistol cartridge. Note that the rim of the case has a smaller diameter than that of the body of the case.
E. A belted 7 mm Remington Magnum rifle cartridge. Note the band of metal at the back of the case, which is used to help seat the cartridge properly in the chamber. Belted cartridges are limited to high-powered rifles.

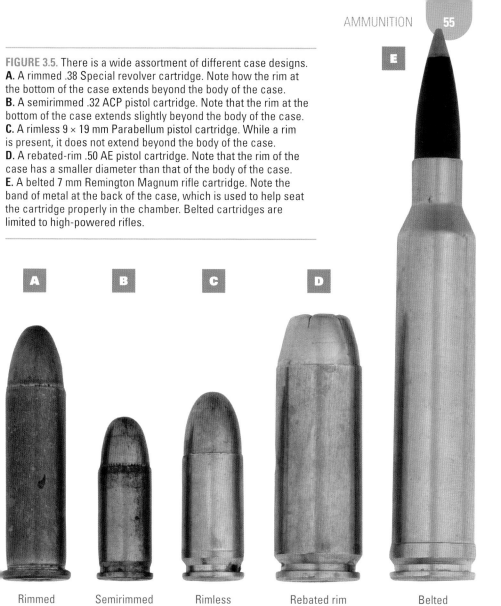

Rimmed   Semirimmed   Rimless   Rebated rim   Belted

HEADSPACE

Headspacing is the distance from whatever portion of the chamber stops the forward movement of the cartridge to whatever seals the breech (this could be part of the slide or it could be the bolt). The five different case types each "headspace" differently. A rimmed cartridge relies solely on the rim to make sure the cartridge is positioned the proper distance into the chamber.

different cartridges with the same caliber of bullet but different case length (.38 Special and .357 Magnum), because the rim ensures that both are held in the proper position.

All rimfire cartridges have rimmed cases, where the priming compound is sandwiched inside the hollow rim.

2. Semirimmed

Semirimmed cases have a small rim that projects slightly beyond the body, along with a recessed groove between the rim and the body (**figure 3.5B**). The rim is large enough to use for headspacing, but not so large as to prevent rounds from effectively stacking in a magazine. While not being an overly common case type, it is used in .32 ACP, .38 ACP, and .38 Super.

3. Rimless

Rimless cases have a base with the same diameter as the body of the case, though the base is separated from the body by a recessed groove (**figure 3.5C**). This groove is used when the empty case needs to be removed from the chamber after the cartridge has been fired. The extractor of the firearm hooks into this groove to pull out the case. With the lack of an overhanging rim, rimless cartridges need something else to ensure proper headspacing. For this purpose, rimless cartridges use the mouth of the case to ensure that they are properly seated in the chamber. If the case has a bottleneck design, sometimes the shoulder of the case is used to help seat it properly.

Rimless cartridges are commonly used for firearms that feed from magazines, since they easily stack on top of one another. Most of the common handgun cartridges are rimless, such as 9 mm Parabellum, .40 S & W, and .45 ACP.

4. Rebated rim

Rebated-rim cases have a rim that is smaller than the diameter of the body of the case (**figure 3.5D**). There is a groove between the rim and the body, which is used for extraction of the case after the round is fired. As with rimless cartridges, cartridges with rebated cases are seated properly from the mouth of the case. Cartridges with rebated rims are not very common, with the large-caliber .50 Action Express (.50 AE) being a notable example.

5. Belted

Belted cases have a thick band of metal at the base (**figure 3.5E**). An extraction groove is milled into the band. The band or "belt" of metal is used to ensure that the cartridge is seated the proper distance into the chamber. Belted cases are used in large "magnum" rifle cartridges such as the .375 Holland & Holland Magnum.

3.1.3. Primer/Pressure-Sensitive Element

Every cartridge has a pressure-sensitive element that, after being struck by the firing pin, will ignite and set off the main gunpowder charge of the round. Modern cartridges are divided into two main types, rimfire and centerfire, differing in the position of the pressure-sensitive element (**figure 3.6A**). Rimfire cartridges have the priming mixture inside the rim, at the base of the cartridge. The firing pin strikes the rim and pinches it together, igniting the priming charge. Since the process physically dents the case, the cases are often discarded and not used for reloading. A centerfire cartridge has a pocket built into the center of the case's base (**figure 3.6B**). This pocket holds a primer, a metal cup with a small priming charge and a rigid piece known as an anvil (**figure 3.6C**). When the firing pin impacts the primer, it dents it and pinches the bottom of the cup into the anvil. The compression of the priming compound causes it to ignite,

FIGURE 3.6. Cartridges have a pressure-sensitive portion that ignites the main gunpowder charge once it is hit by the firing pin. **A.** Centerfire and rimfire cartridges differ in their placement of the pressure-sensitive element. A centerfire cartridge has a separate primer that holds the priming compound. A rimfire cartridge has the priming compound sandwiched inside the rim of the case. **B.** A primer sits in a pocket at the base of a centerfire cartridge. To the left is a .45 ACP case with the primer removed, showing the primer pocket. To the right is a .45 ACP case with a primer still inserted. The primer is dented, indicating that the cartridge has been fired. **C.** The bottom (*left*) and top (*right*) views of a primer. When the firing pin strikes the primer, the impact crushes the priming compound into an anvil inside the primer. Part of the anvil can be seen in the top view of the primer. A dime is included for scale.

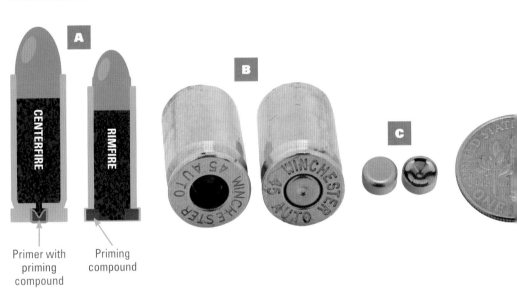

Primer with priming compound

Priming compound

sending a spark through a flash hole into the case. There are two main primer designs: Boxer and Berdan. Cartridges using Boxer primers have a single flash hole in the base of the case, whereas cartridges using Berdan primers have two flash holes.

3.1.4. Powder

Black powder was the earliest form of gunpowder developed, though it is no longer used in most modern cartridges. Black powder is a mixture of sulfur, charcoal, and potassium nitrate (saltpeter) that when burned creates a substantial amount of heat and a buildup of gas pressure to propel bullets. Aside from releasing hot gas, the combustion of black powder also yields a substantial amount of smoke and solid byproducts that collect in the gun barrel. Black powder is classified on the basis of the size of the powder granules. The larger the granules, the slower the powder will burn. This is often designated with a series of the letter "F." The greater the number of Fs, the finer the granule size (**figure 3.7A**). FFFF has finer granules than FFF, which has finer granules than FF, etc. Finer granules are usually used in the flash pan of a flintlock firearm, while courser granules are used for the main powder charge behind the bullet. The Fs are usually followed by the letter *g*, which indicates that the powder is for sporting (shooting) applications, whereas a-grade powder is used for blasting in quarries.

The Bureau of Alcohol, Tobacco, Firearms, and Explosives (ATF) classifies black powder as an explosive, though it is considered a "low" explosive. Explosives are categorized by the

FIGURE 3.7. Modern firearms use a type of gunpowder called smokeless powder. **A.** A container of black powder (*left*) and a container of smokeless powder (*right*). The three Fs on the black-powder container indicate that the powder granules are finely ground. **B.** Granules of FFFg black powder (*left*) and discs of smokeless powder (*right*). A dime is included for scale.

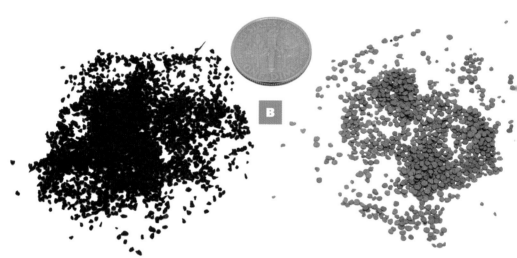

speed at which the combustion reaction proceeds. A "low" explosive undergoes the process of deflagration, where the combustion reaction is spread by the flame traveling through the explosive substance and igniting it. While this process is rapid, it happens at a speed below the speed of sound. Most fires encountered in everyday life are deflagrations. A "high" explosive detonates, where a shock wave travels through the explosive substance at speeds faster than the speed of sound, causing the combustion reaction to spread. Trinitrotoluene (TNT) and dynamite are examples of high explosives.

Modern cartridges use smokeless powder, though the name is something of a misnomer, since it still produces smoke during combustion, just significantly less than black powder. When smokeless powder burns, nearly all the products of combustion are gas, so the firearm barrel is not coated with solid residue like with black powder. Modern smokeless powders are composed of nitrocellulose, with some containing nitroglycerine. As with black powder, smokeless powder does not detonate—it deflagrates; however, it does burn at a more controlled rate than black powder. Smokeless powder is generally granular, though sometimes it takes the form of flattened spheres, and it takes up less space than black powder (**figure 3.7B**). Many older revolver cartridges designed for black powder are now loaded with smokeless powder, such that a large portion of the case is not filled. If you are interested in loading your own cartridges from the separate components, it is essential that you use the appropriate powder. Using black powder in the place of smokeless powder can have disastrous consequences.

3.2. Naming Conventions

The naming conventions used for cartridges can be a significant source of confusion when one is starting to shoot handguns. Unfortunately, there is not a standard naming convention, which leads to a lot of the confusion.

One of the main ways of differentiating cartridges is by the caliber. Caliber is an approximation of the diameter of the bore of the firearm, or the diameter of the bullet it fires. It is always a number, either in millimeters (mm) or in inches. This disparity in the measuring convention is due to the United States not adopting the metric system. A .45-caliber bullet has an approximate diameter of 0.45 inches, but depending on what specific cartridge it is used in, the exact value will vary at the thousandths decimal place. As an example, .45 ACP cartridge (**figure 3.8A**) has a bullet with the diameter of 0.452 inches, a .45 Schofield has a bullet diameter of 0.454 inches (**figure 3.8B**), a .45 Colt (**figure 3.8C**) has a bullet with the diameter of 0.454 inches, and a .454 Casull (**figure 3.8D**) has the bullet diameter of 0.452.* It should be noted that these dimensions can slightly change depending on whether you are using lead bullets or jacketed bullets.

* F. C. Barnes, *Cartridges of the World*, 15th ed.,
(Iola, Wisconsin: Gun Digest Books, 2016), p. 681.

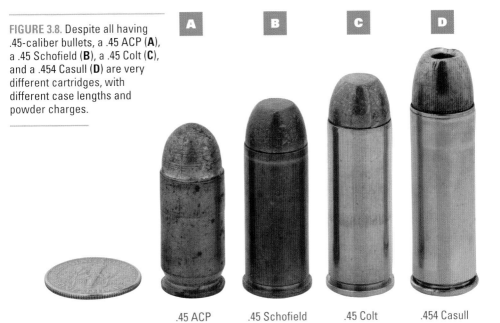

FIGURE 3.8. Despite all having .45-caliber bullets, a .45 ACP (**A**), a .45 Schofield (**B**), a .45 Colt (**C**), and a .454 Casull (**D**) are very different cartridges, with different case lengths and powder charges.

.45 ACP   .45 Schofield   .45 Colt   .454 Casull

Since there are often multiple cartridges using the same caliber, cartridges need some additional notation to help differentiate them. For many American cartridges, the caliber will be followed by some other descriptor, such as the name of the company that developed it (.40 Smith & Wesson), the name of the inventor (.454 Casull), or the type of firearm it was developed for (.45 ACP for Automatic Colt Pistol).

Most European cartridges are designated by two numbers, the caliber of the bullet and then the length of the case in millimeters: [bullet diameter] × [case length]. If you were to name the .45 ACP (**figure 3.8A**) by using the European convention, it would be called 11.43 × 23 mm, with 11.43 being the diameter of the bullet in millimeters, and 23 mm being the length of the case. The .45 Colt (**figure 3.8C**), sometimes colloquially known as .45 Long Colt, would be designated as 11.43 × 33 mmR. This means that a .45 Colt has a bullet with the diameter of 11.43 mm, and a case with the length of 33 mm. The "R" in 33 mmR stands for "rimmed," since the base is rimmed.

One of the most commonly used European cartridges today is the 9 × 19 mm Parabellum. It has a bullet with a diameter of 9 mm and a case with the length of 19 mm (**figure 3.9C**). The cartridge is also known as 9 mm Luger because it was designed by the Austrian designer Georg Luger. Furthermore, the cartridge is colloquially known as 9 mm, despite there being a plethora of other cartridges that have a metric caliber of 9 mm (**table 3.1**). As an example, the Russian cartridge 9 × 18 mm Makarov also has a 9 mm bullet, but it has a case that is 1 mm shorter (**figure 3.9B**). The bullet has a slightly larger diameter (0.365" compared to 0.355") as well. Because of these two differences, you cannot fire a 9 × 18 mm Makarov cartridge in a handgun designed to shoot 9 × 19 mm Parabellum. Additionally, .380 ACP, a common defensive cartridge, has a 9 mm bullet but a 17 mm long case (**figure 3.9A**).

9 x 17mm
.380 ACP

9 x 18mm
Makarov

9 x 19mm
Parabellum

FIGURE 3.9. There are a wide range of cartridges that use a 9 mm bullet, but they have different case lengths and amounts of gunpowder. **A.** .380 ACP, or 9 × 17 mm, is a popular self-defense cartridge with a 9 mm bullet. **B.** 9 × 18 Makarov is a Russian pistol cartridge that uses a 9 mm bullet with a case length 1 mm longer than .380 ACP. **C.** 9 × 19 mm Parabellum, or 9 mm Luger, is one of the most popular 9 mm cartridges. It is often referred to simply as 9 mm, though that can be misleading. A dime has been included for scale.

Table 3.1. Common Handgun Calibers in Inches and Millimeters

Information from F. C. Barnes, *Cartridges of the World*, 15th ed., Iola, Wisconsin: Gun Digest Books, 2016.

CALIBER (INCHES)	METRIC CALIBER	BULLET DIAMETER	COMMON CARTRIDGES
0.22	5.6 mm	0.223 in.	.22 Short, .22 Long, .22 Long Rifle
0.355	9 mm	0.355 in.	9 × 19 mm Parabellum (9 mm Luger)
0.356	9 mm	0.356 in.	.380 ACP
0.357	9 mm	0.357 in.	.38 Special, .357 Magnum
0.363	9 mm	0.363 in.	9 × 18 mm Makarov
0.40	10 mm	0.400 in.	.40 S & W, 10 mm Auto
0.44	10.9 mm	0.429 in.	.44 Remington Magnum
0.45	11.43 mm	0.452–0.454 in.	.45 ACP, .45 GAP, .454 Casull, .45 Colt
0.50	12.7 mm	0.500 in.	.50 Action Express

Common Cartridges*

.22 Long Rifle: The .22 Long Rifle is a rimfire cartridge that is used both in pistols and rifles and is one of the most popular cartridges in the world. Due to its small-caliber bullet and relatively low amount of gunpowder, it has very little felt recoil when fired. This makes it an excellent choice for introducing people to shooting. Newcomers will often anticipate the recoil of a firearm and unintentionally jerk the gun as they are pressing the trigger. The negligible recoil of a .22 Long Rifle largely alleviates this problem.

9 x 19 mm Parabellum: One of the most popular small-arms cartridges in the world, the 9 × 19 mm Parabellum was designed by Georg Luger in 1902 for the Luger semiautomatic pistol. Because of this, the cartridge is also commonly known as the 9 mm Luger. In the United States, this cartridge is colloquially known as "9 mm," ignoring the notion that there are many cartridges with 9 mm caliber bullets. It was adopted by the US military in 1985, when the Beretta M9 semiautomatic pistol was selected as their primary sidearm, replacing the .45 ACP M1911A1.

.380 ACP: The .380 ACP (Automatic Colt Pistol) is a rimless cartridge designed by John Browning in 1908 for a hammerless, semiautomatic pistol to be concealed in a vest pocket. The cartridge name via the European convention is 9 × 17 mm, so it is very similar to 9 × 19 mm Parabellum, with a slightly shorter case. The cartridge goes by many other names, including 9 mm Short, 9 mm Kurz (German), 9 mm Corto (Spanish), and 9 mm Browning-Court (French). It is a very popular cartridge for concealed-carry handguns.

.38 Super: The .38 Super is a semirimmed pistol cartridge that was developed by taking the .38 ACP (not to be confused with the .380 ACP) cartridge and adding additional gunpowder to increase bullet velocity. Though it was designed in the late 1920s, the cartridge did not become popular until the 1980s, when it began to see usage in pistol-shooting competitions.

.38 Special: The .38 Special is a rimmed revolver cartridge that was developed by Smith & Wesson in 1902 to replace the unsuccessful .38 Long Colt employed by the United States Army. The cartridge had a long history as the standard service cartridge for many police departments up until the 1990s. The name implies that the cartridge has a .38-inch diameter, but it is actually .357 inches. The .38 inches comes from the diameter of the fully loaded cartridge. A .38 Special and a .357 Magnum cartridge differ only in the case length and amount of gunpowder, with the .38 Special having a shorter case and less powder. Being shorter and less charged, .38 Special cartridges can be loaded and fired through most .357 Magnum revolvers. The same cannot be said in reverse, however. You should not attempt to fire .357 Magnum cartridges in a revolver specifically chambered for .38 Special. In most cases, a .357 Magnum will not fit into a revolver that was designed to only shoot .38 Special cartridges.

.357 Magnum: The .357 Magnum is a rimmed revolver cartridge designed around the .38 Special. It has the same caliber of bullet, though it has additional gunpowder and a longer case. In actuality, the longer case is not needed to contain the additional gunpowder. It was included for safety purposes to make sure they were not loaded in a .38 Special revolver, which was not designed to withstand the increased pressures of the .357 Magnum.

.40 S & W: The .40 S & W is a rimless pistol cartridge developed by Smith & Wesson and Winchester in 1990 for the Federal Bureau of Investigation (FBI). After a 1986 shootout between two bank robbers and eight FBI agents left two agents dead and five wounded, the FBI began to search for a replacement for their .38 Special service revolvers. They were looking to switch from the revolver to a semiautomatic pistol due to its speed of reloading and increased ammunition capacity. The .40 S & W was developed from the powerful 10 mm Auto cartridge, lowering the amount of gunpowder and shortening the case but keeping the bullet diameter and case width the same. With the cartridge being smaller than the 10 mm Auto, it could fit into a smaller-framed pistol, similar to a 9 × 19 mm, but still retain some of the stopping power of the 10 mm Auto.

.45 ACP: The .45 ACP (Automatic Colt Pistol) is a rimless pistol cartridge designed by John Browning in 1905. It was developed to replace the .38 Long Colt, which the US military had been using as its standard pistol cartridge since 1892. Specifically, they were looking for something with more stopping power. In 1911, the United States selected the M1911 pistol as its official sidearm, chambered in .45 ACP. The cartridge has a substantial stopping power against human targets with a moderate recoil, but because of the cartridge's large size, magazine capacity is lower than with other smaller rounds. There are high-capacity .45 ACP handguns, but in order to accommodate this, the thickness of the handle needs to be increased, which can make them difficult to hold properly if you have small hands.

---

[*] Information from F. C. Barnes, *Cartridges of the World*, 15th ed., Iola, Wisconsin: Gun Digest Books, 2016.

3.3. Standard-Pressure and Overpressure Ammunition

When a cartridge is fired, there is a short period of time when a large amount of pressure builds up inside the chamber of the gun, which forces the bullet out of the barrel. Firearm barrels are designed to withstand greater pressures than what a standard cartridge will produce. In fact, before a firearm can be sold, a "proof" round is fired through it, which is deliberately loaded with more gunpowder than normal to create substantially larger pressures in the chamber. This is done to confirm that the barrel is not defective and to make sure that it does not explode. The Sporting Arms and Ammunition Manufacturers' Institute (SAAMI) publishes standards for acceptable chamber pressures for every cartridge, and standards for proof rounds for each cartridge. While each barrel is designed to withstand these proof rounds, they are not designed to continually withstand such high pressures.

A number of common cartridges used for defensive purposes are deliberately loaded with more gunpowder than normal to increase the pressure (these rounds always have less gunpowder than the proof round, however), and therefore the velocity of the fired bullet. This overpressure ammunition is conventionally referred to as "plus pressure," or +P. SAAMI sets guidelines for +P ammunition, where the pressure is approximately 10 percent higher

FIGURE 3.10. Plus pressure (+P) ammunition is loaded with additional gunpowder to increase the velocity of the bullet when it is fired. **A.** A box of .38 Special cartridges (*on the left*) and a box of .38 Special +P cartridges (*on the right*). Ammunition packaging will clearly label whether the ammunition is +P. **B.** Pictured here are two regular .38 Special cartridges, one upright and one on its side (*left*), and two .38 Special + P cartridges, one upright and one on its side (*right*). The base of each case has been magnified for readability. The bottom of the cases will be stamped with the cartridge type, including whether it is +P.

---

than that of the standard load. Aside from +P, there is also +P+ ammunition, which has higher pressures than +P. It is important that you make sure that your handgun is designed to fire +P or +P+ ammunition before using it; otherwise it might not hold up to continual use of +P ammunition. The packaging for the ammunition will say whether it is +P ammunition or not (**figure 3.10A**). The bottom of the cartridge case will also say whether the ammunition is +P (**figure 3.10B**).

3.4. Safety Considerations

As mentioned in section 1.2, it is imperative that you are using the proper ammunition in your handgun. The cartridge name will be stamped at the base of each cartridge, and it will be clearly printed on the packaging of the ammunition. This needs to match exactly with what is stamped onto the barrel or slide of your handgun. Since there are multiple different cartridges with the same caliber of bullets, you need to make sure your ammunition matches exactly with your firearm, since most handguns are specifically designed to fire only a single cartridge.

3.4.1. Cartridge Malfunctions

Most commercially loaded ammunition is of high quality, and you will not often run into problems with it. Regardless of this, it is important to be aware of potential ammunition malfunctions so that you can recognize them if they come up. There are three types of cartridge malfunctions that you should be cognizant of: hangfire, misfire, and squib.

Hangfire

A hangfire occurs when you pull the trigger to fire a round and there is a delay before the cartridge ignites. The primer is impacted, and, due to a defective primer or gunpowder, it takes a few seconds before it ignites the main gunpowder charge to propel the bullet out of the barrel. This is most common with extremely old ammunition. If you pull the trigger and the cartridge is not fired, keep the firearm pointed in a safe direction and wait for thirty seconds to see if ignition is delayed. If after thirty seconds there is still no ignition, you likely have a misfire.

Misfire

If you are shooting and pull the trigger, and no round appears to fire, you could be experiencing a misfire. With a misfire, the firing pin strikes the primer, or the rim, and the cartridge fails to ignite. This is caused either by a defect in the cartridge or by a damaged firing pin that does not fully strike the cartridge. If you pull the trigger and the cartridge does not ignite, make sure the firearm is pointing in a safe direction and wait for thirty seconds to see if you are experiencing a hangfire. If after thirty seconds there is no ignition, unload the handgun. If it is a semiautomatic, remove the magazine and then pull the slide back to eject the round. Inspect the cartridge to see if the primer or rim has been dented. If it looks to have been normally dented, you should try to fire the cartridge again and see if it will fire. If it does not, it is an issue with the primer/priming compound. If the primer appears not to have been dented or is only partially dented, there could be something amiss with the firing pin or striker of your handgun (and thus it is actually a mechanical problem).

Squib

A squib is when a cartridge does not have enough powder to propel the bullet out of the gun. After igniting the cartridge, sufficient pressure does not build up to have the bullet clear the barrel, and it remains lodged inside the barrel. This can be very dangerous if you do not notice it happening and fire another round, launching it directly into the one still in the bore (**figure 3.11**). You need to pay close attention to the sound and recoil of your shots. If something seems amiss, such as lower noise, recoil, or muzzle flash, you may have experienced a squib. If you suspect a squib, stop firing and make sure you keep the gun pointed in a safe direction. Unload the handgun and make sure that the chamber is empty. Run a cleaning rod through the barrel to see if it is obstructed with a bullet. If a bullet is lodged in the barrel, you should remove it with the assistance of a brass rod, aluminum rod, or wooden dowel rod and a rubber mallet. Steel can scratch the bore and should not be used. If the barrel can be removed from the frame, like with many semiautomatic pistols, you should remove it first. It is a good idea to keep a brass rod and a rubber mallet in your range bag when you go shooting, in case this problem arises.

FIGURE 3.11. Squib rounds can be very dangerous if not noticed. This is the barrel of a Glock pistol that had two squibs fired into it, before both were shot out of the barrel with a third round. The barrel now has a significant bulge in it and is unusable. Fortunately, this incident ended without anyone getting hurt, but such an incident could rupture the barrel because of the huge spike in pressure.

Bulge in barrel

Squibs are very uncommon in commercially loaded ammunition and happen most often with people who reload their cartridges and accidentally leave the powder charge out of one of them. If you have loaded a cartridge with a primer and bullet but no gunpowder, the primer might have enough power to launch the bullet into the barrel.

ASIDE:

The strategies described above for handling an ammunition malfunction are ideal, though many experienced shooters do not wait thirty seconds to see if they have a misfire or a hangfire. While keeping the gun pointed in a safe direction, they will tap the magazine to see if it is inserted properly, and then pull back the slide to eject the round in question. With the exception of having a squib, this will ready the gun to continue shooting. The ejected round can then be examined afterward to determine if the primer was dented. This general strategy is known as "Tap, Rack, and Go" in some circles and is the suggested method to surmount potential problems when in a defensive situation. This is discussed in more detail in section 6.3.1.

3.5. Reloading

Ammunition can be very expensive, and with rising prices of metal worldwide, that is never going to change. This can severely limit the amount of time that a person can spend shooting their handgun. As a means to save money, some individuals will load their own cartridges by hand, using the individual components (reloading). It is important to note that reloading can be an expensive hobby since it requires specialized equipment to perform **(figure 3.12)**. It is unlikely that you will save money reloading, but it will allow you to shoot more often which will help improve your shooting abilities.

There are a number of reasons to consider reloading:

- It will enable you to shoot more often.

- It allows you to prepare cartridges with a specific amount of gunpowder that functions particularly well in your handgun.

- You can prepare cartridges that are difficult to find in stores. There are many obscure cartridges that are no longer popular and might not be commercially available.

- It is a fun and enjoyable challenge.

In a general sense, a person who loads their own cartridges is recycling the brass cases from rounds that they have already fired. After shooting, a reloader will pick up the brass cases of the cartridges that they fired and prepare them to be used again. Only cases from centerfire cartridges can be reused, and only if they are brass or nickel plated. The collected brass cases are prepared for reuse by removing the spent primer, resizing the case to factory specifications, and inserting a new primer. Gunpowder is added to the cases next. The amount of gunpowder and the type, is detailed in a plethora of reloading manuals that are commercially available. Lyman, Hornady, RCBS, and Speer all have good offerings. Lyman is a particularly good choice because they include lead-cast bullet data, and, since they do not make their own bullets, the book is not biased toward any particular products. The other manuals include load data specifically for their bullet types. The gunpowder specifications and amounts in the manuals need to be followed very carefully and exactly, lest you overload a cartridge and risk blowing apart your gun from excessive pressure buildup. After adding the gunpowder, a bullet is seated into the mouth of the case. The depth of the bullet placement is discussed in the reloading manual. After inserting the bullet to the proper depth, some cartridges need the mouth of the case to be pinched around the bullet, a process known as crimping. With that, the cartridges are ready to be used. This a general overview of the reloading process and is not intended to take the place of reading an actual book or taking a course on reloading.

FIGURE 3.12. Reloading cartridges requires a lot of equipment and knowledge. The equipment on the pictured bench is as follows, *from left to right:* a single-stage press (sometimes called a rock chucker) in green, which is the most basic reloading unit, a container of smokeless powder, and a Lyman Reloading manual. Behind the reloading manual is a Dillon Square Deal progressive press for loading straight-walled cartridges. A digital scale for weighing gunpowder (*middle right*) and a plastic container with empty cases (*far right*). A Hornady Lock-N-Load progressive press in red (*top right*).

RUGER GP100®

.357 MAGNUM CAL.

HOW TO CHOOSE
A HANDGUN

CHAPTER 4 HOW TO CHOOSE A HANDGUN

Walking into a gun shop with the intent to purchase your first handgun can be an overwhelming experience. The sheer number of different firearms and options available to you is staggering (**figure 4.1**). A lot of this feeling can be alleviated if you know how you intend to use the handgun. There are many different applications for handguns, and, as such, there are many different types of handguns to meet those needs. Knowing what you are interested in using it for will help you greatly in deciding on something that is right for you. No single gun will be perfect for every application. If you are primarily concerned with shooting for leisure, your criteria will be different than for someone who is interested in something concealable for self-defense.

FIGURE 4.1. Your first trip to a gun shop can be overwhelming due to the vast number of choices available to you.

4.1. General Aspects That Affect Firearm Performance

Before going into detail about what makes a handgun ideal for sporting or what makes one ideal for concealment, there are a number of aspects that influence their performance that need to be discussed, including (1) barrel length, (2) fit in hand, (3) natural point of aim, and (4) ammunition. Regardless of your intended use for a handgun, these are aspects that you should consider.

4.1.1. Barrel Length

As a general rule of thumb, longer-barreled handguns are easier to shoot well than their shorter-barreled brethren. There are a number of reasons for this, but the one that plays the largest role is sight radius. Simply put, sight radius is the distance between the front and rear sights on a firearm. With a longer barrel, the sight radius is longer, which makes it easier to detect errors in sight alignment. Being able to notice and correct these alignment errors can have a considerable effect on accuracy. Increasing the barrel length and the sight radius will generally help with accuracy, so long as you can still easily focus on the front sight. A long barrel is of little value if you cannot easily focus on the front sight. This becomes evident as a person's eyes get older and they become less able to focus on distant objects. Because of this, older shooters often find that they are more successful with shorter-barreled handguns. It is important to realize that longer-barreled handguns are not inherently more accurate than shorter-barreled handguns; it is just easier to detect your own misalignments with a longer sight radius and then correct for them.

Aside from having a longer sight radius, a longer barrel helps impart additional stabilization to the bullet as it travels down the length of the barrel. As described in section 2.1, the bore of most modern firearms is lined with helical grooves known as rifling. When the firearm is fired and the bullet is propelled out of the barrel, the rifling imparts spin on the bullet, such that it exits the barrel on a straight path. A longer barrel allows for increased bullet stabilization, which in turn improves accuracy. Before the advent of rifling, firearms had smooth bores and were not as accurate.

ASIDE:

Stabilizing a projectile by applying spin to it has been around since the time of the bow and arrow. To make sure that arrows flew straight, fletching was applied to the back end of each arrow shaft. Fletching usually consists of three equally spaced fins around the circumference of the arrow shaft, which would help spin the arrow in flight.

4.1.2. Fit in Hand

Another important characteristic to consider when choosing a handgun is how it fits in your hand. The best way to determine this is by actually feeling and handling the firearm. A particularly important characteristic to consider is the distance between the top of the backstrap of the handle and the trigger. Generally, your index finger should contact the trigger between the tip and the first joint (see section 5.2.2.4 for more detail). You want to find a handgun with a handle thickness that allows you to easily do this. If the handle is too thick for your hand, you will often modify your grip on the gun, rotating it such that your index finger can reach the trigger properly. This changes the axis of the barrel of the gun relative to your arm, bringing it out of alignment with your forearm. Normally, you want the handgun to be lined up with your forearm, allowing the recoil to be absorbed by your arm. If you have to alter your grip to properly reach the trigger, the recoil of the gun will likely be absorbed into your thumb, which is unpleasant and distracting (see section 5.1.1 for more information about holding a handgun properly). Ultimately, you want to choose a handgun that is pleasant to shoot; otherwise, shooting will not be the enjoyable experience that it should be.

4.1.3. Natural Point of Aim

Your natural point of aim is the position that you instinctively adopt when you bring up a handgun to aim. Determining your natural aiming position is a simple process:

Hold your handgun in a two-handed grip and point it toward the ground (**figure 4.2A**). This is called the "low ready" position (see section 5.1.2 for a more complete description). Now, close your eyes and bring the gun up to the shooting position. Open your eyes and take note of where the handgun is positioned (**figure 4.2B**). This is your natural point of aim. Your brain determined that this was the most comfortable position to adopt.

Ideally, this natural position will result in the gun having its sights aligned fairly well. If they are not, you will have to expend additional effort to move the gun to align the sights. You can try modifying your stance and doing the exercise again to see if the alignment improves. When choosing a handgun, you should find one that you can aim naturally and not have to do too many adjustments to align the sights on target.

FIGURE 4.2. Your natural point of aim is where your body intuitively positions your handgun when you bring it up to aim. **A.** To determine your natural point of aim, adopt a comfortable shooting stance, with the handgun pointed downrange and toward the floor. **B.** Close your eyes and then bring the gun into a comfortable shooting position. This is your natural point of aim.

As a general point, when aiming a handgun, you want to bring the handgun up to your eyes, and not lower your eyes to find the gun. It makes target acquisition faster, and it allows you to be more consistent.

4.1.4. Ammunition

Barrel length and the ergonomics of the handgun are important when deciding on what to buy, but the cartridge that the gun fires is also very important. Choosing the proper cartridge can have a profound impact on your shooting for two primary reasons: (1) the recoil associated with the cartridge can affect your performance, and (2) the price of the ammunition can be prohibitive if you choose a more expensive cartridge. Each of these points deserves some additional explanation.

4.1.4.1. Recoil

Anyone with even a rudimentary knowledge of firearms is aware of the "kick" associated with firing them. This "kick," or recoil, is the backward momentum of the firearm after discharging it, which balances the forward momentum of the bullet leaving the gun. Sir Isaac Newton was referring to this notion when he said that "every action has an equal and opposite reaction." Another way of visualizing this concept is to imagine stepping out of a boat onto a dock. When you step out onto the dock, the boat pushes away from you. As your legs move you toward the dock, they provide an opposite force backward, pushing the boat away from you.

The recoil of a firearm is in direct response to the momentum of the bullet going in the opposite direction (forward momentum). The bullet's momentum (p_{bullet}) is the product of its mass (m_{bullet}) multiplied by its velocity (v_{bullet}):

$$p_{bullet} = m_{bullet} * v_{bullet}$$

Since momentum needs to be conserved, the momentum of the bullet (p_{bullet}) is accompanied by an equal momentum of the gun (p_{gun}), just that it is directed backward:

$$p_{bullet} = -p_{gun}$$

The numerical values of the momentums are the same (they are equal), but since the gun's momentum is directed in the opposite direction of the bullet, it has a negative value.

Some worthwhile insights can come from considering what constitutes these two momentums, and how they differ, despite having equal values. Recall that momentum (p) is the product of multiplying mass (m) of an object by its velocity (v):

$$p = m*v$$

Substituting p for $m*v$ in $p_{bullet} = -p_{gun}$ gives $m_{bullet}*v_{bullet} = -m_{gun}*v_{gun}$.

A bullet by itself does not have a considerable mass (m_{bullet}), but it leaves the barrel of the gun at an extremely high velocity (v_{bullet}). Together, their product results in a considerable forward momentum (**figure 4.3**). The gun is propelled backward with an equal momentum, satisfying Newton's third law. While the momentums are equal, the masses and velocities of each are different (**figure 4.3**). The firearm has a considerably greater mass (m_{gun}) than the bullet (m_{bullet}), allowing for it to have much smaller backward velocity (v_{gun}). It would be a serious problem for the shooter if the handgun was projected backward at the same velocity as the bullet leaving the gun.

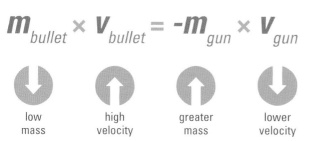

$$m_{bullet} \times v_{bullet} = -m_{gun} \times v_{gun}$$

low mass	high velocity	greater mass	lower velocity

FIGURE 4.3. The momentum of a bullet leaving a gun is equal to the momentum of the gun recoiling backward, but the components that make up these momentums differ. Here, the momentum of the bullet and the gun is represented as their components: their mass (*m*) and velocity (*v*) multiplied together. The mass of a bullet is low (*downward arrow*), but it leaves the barrel of a gun at a high velocity (*upward arrow*). The momentum of the gun is equal to that of the bullet, but the gun has a much greater mass than the bullet. Because of this, the velocity of the gun moving backward has to be lower than the velocity of the bullet. The negative sign associated with the right half of the equation denotes that the momentum of the gun is in the opposite direction of the bullet.

If a handgun has a considerable recoil, it can start to negatively affect your accuracy. You will often anticipate the recoil and preemptively flinch while pulling the trigger. This upsets your aim and leads to accuracy problems.

A general understanding of recoil makes it clear that it is influenced by many factors. It is primarily determined by four things: (1) the caliber of the cartridge, (2) the weight of the gun, (3) the barrel length of the gun, and (4) the grip surface on the gun.

1. Caliber

Caliber is the bore diameter of the firearm, which largely corresponds to the diameter of a bullet in a cartridge as well. As an example, a .45 ACP bullet has a diameter of 0.451 inches. The higher the caliber, the larger the bullet, and the greater the mass. Increasing the mass of the bullet will help increase the momentum of the bullet, which has to be matched by the momentum of the gun recoiling in the opposite direction. While this is a simplification of the physics involved, the larger the round a firearm shoots, the greater the recoil.

2. Weight of gun

The greater the mass of the gun, the lower the gun's velocity will be to match the momentum of the bullet. Because of this, small and lighter guns often have more recoil than larger guns. Small handguns that were made for concealment are often not very pleasant to shoot because they have such a small mass.

To return to the "stepping out of the boat" analogy used earlier, if you were stepping onto a dock from a canoe, as opposed to a larger rowboat, it would push away from the dock faster because of its smaller mass.

3. Barrel length of the gun

Generally, handguns with longer barrels have less recoil than those with shorter barrels. This is simply a function of the additional barrel length adding more mass to the gun, allowing the velocity of the gun to be lower.

4. Grip surface on the gun

The more of your hand that you have clasped around the handle of the handgun, the more control you have over it. If you have the entirety of your hand around the firearm, each finger in place, it will not lurch as much in your hand upon firing it (**figure 4.4A**). This will

FIGURE 4.4. The more complete your grasp of the handgun, the better control you will have over the recoil. **A.** Larger handguns have a bigger grip surface, allowing a place for each of your fingers. **B.** Small handguns designed for concealment have small handles that do not offer space for each of your fingers. Folding your thumb beneath the grip can add some extra stability.

result in less felt recoil. Handguns designed for concealment often have truncated handles, some of which do not have space for all your fingers (**figure 4.4B**). This limited grip surface makes it harder to keep the handgun from moving when shooting it. Many of these handguns will have larger magazines that add additional grip surface to the handgun. Of course, by extending the magazine, you are forfeiting the gains in concealability that a shorter handle provided.

4.1.4.2. Price of Ammunition

The recoil associated with a cartridge is not the only thing you should consider when deciding what handgun to purchase. The cost of ammunition can have a significant impact on how often you are able to shoot your handgun. If you are buying your first handgun, it is beneficial to purchase one that shoots a cartridge that is affordable to shoot regularly. After all, the best way to become proficient at shooting is with practice. **Table 4.1** lists some of the popular pistol cartridges and their cost per round (as of 2017). While larger and more-powerful cartridges might seem appealing, shooting them is considerably more expensive.

Table 4.1. Breakdown of popular pistol cartridges and their cost by individual round. Costs are based on an average of prices at Enck's Gun Barn, June 2019.

CARTRIDGE	COST PER ROUND ($)
.22 Long Rifle (.22 LR)	0.06
9 × 19 mm Parabellum (commonly called 9 mm)	0.24
.380 ACP	0.34
.38 Special	0.40
.40 S&W	0.31
.45 ACP	0.40

4.2. What Is Your Intended Use for the Handgun?

The number of different handguns on the market is vast, each designed with a specific task in mind. No handgun is going to be the perfect choice for every application. To help clear up some of the confusion, handguns can be classified into two main types: carry guns and range guns. Carry guns are those that are ideal for hiding on your person for self-defense. They are usually small and light, making them easy to conceal. Range guns are larger and designed to be easy to shoot accurately. These larger sizes make concealing them a challenge. No firearm is going to perfectly fit into both categories.

4.2.1. Carry Gun

If you are intending to conceal a firearm on your person and carry it around on a daily basis, you want something that is small and lightweight. If it is fairly large, it will greatly influence the type of clothing that you need to wear to keep it hidden. In an effort to make concealing easy, most concealment guns have short barrels. Many are very light because their frames are made of polymer, as opposed to metal. All these things make the gun easier to hide on your person, but they contribute to making them harder to shoot well.

As mentioned in section 4.1.1, shorter-barreled handguns are often harder to shoot effectively. Since they are small, some do not have a large enough handle to allow room for each finger of your hand, especially if you have large hands. This makes it harder to control the recoil of the firearm. And since they usually have low-weight polymer frames, the shooter feels more of the recoil (see section 4.1.4.1). All these aspects are summed up with the phrase "Little and cute isn't fun to shoot." Smaller handguns might be convenient for concealing, but they have more recoil associated with them and are not as pleasant to shoot.

4.2.2. Range Gun

A range gun is not designed to be concealed, so they are larger and heavier. They often have longer barrels, which make them easier to shoot. They usually have full-sized frames, giving your hand more room for holding them. The full-sized frames and longer barrels contribute to more weight and help lessen the felt recoil when shooting them. Some will also have adjustable sights, allowing the shooter to calibrate their gun for shooting at specific distances. It should be noted that handguns with nonadjustable, "fixed" sights have their sights specifically calibrated for one distance.

If you are buying a handgun largely for leisure shooting, you do not want to buy a small firearm meant for concealment. Concealment guns are not designed to be pleasurably shot all afternoon at a shooting range. The recoil will start to hurt your hand and wrist, and you will probably have trouble shooting it as effectively as you would like, unless you are an experienced shooter.

4.2.3. Buying a Handgun Is an Exercise in Compromise

When you are considering buying a handgun, your purchase should be guided by your intended use for the gun, since no single gun will be perfect for every application. Imagine that every handgun falls into a continuum, ranging from a dedicated range gun to a dedicated carry gun (**figure 4.5**). You can easily place most guns into this continuum by just looking at their size. Smaller guns are carry guns, and larger ones are range guns. There are a disorienting number of different handguns available, but by just looking at their size, you can determine the basic function of most of them. Handguns that fit in the middle of the continuum combine aspects both of range guns and carry guns, with varying levels of success.

ASIDE: BUYING A MILITARY SURPLUS HANDGUN CAN BE A GOOD WAY TO GET INTO SHOOTING.

Instead of looking at new firearms for your first handgun, you could also consider getting a military surplus handgun. These are handguns that saw use by military personnel or police forces around the world but are no longer used for active service. Many of these are excellently produced handguns with production values that would be very expensive to reproduce in today's industry. These handguns can serve as an excellent way to economically enter the world of handgun shooting. Since all of these are old firearms, it can be difficult to find replacement parts if something breaks.

It should be noted that many of these firearms use more-uncommon ammunition, such as 9 × 18 mm Makarov or 7.62 × 25 mm Tokarev. A sizable portion of these firearms have magazine releases at the base of the grip, behind the magazine well. This makes removing the magazine a little more challenging, with the hope that it would make it more likely that soldiers would retain their magazines.

Notable choices:

1. **P64:** A Polish semiautomatic pistol chambered in 9 × 18 mm Makarov.

2. **FEG P63:** A Hungarian semiautomatic pistol that borrows many designs from the Walther PPK. It is chambered in 9 × 18 mm Makarov.

3. **TT-30/TT-33:** The TT-30 is a Russian semiautomatic pistol chambered in 7.62 × 25 mm Tokarev. The TT-33 (**figure 4.6A**) is a slightly modified version of the same firearm to assist in ease of manufacturing. The TT-33 was produced by many other countries, often adopting different names. As an example, Zastava Arms from Serbia produces an improved version of the TT-33 called the M57.

4. **CZ 52 / CZ 82:** The CZ 52 (**figure 4.6B**) is a Czechoslovakian semiautomatic handgun chambered in 7.62 × 25 mm Tokarev. The CZ 52 was replaced by the CZ 82, which fires 9 × 18 Makarov (**figure 4.6C**).

5. **Star Model BM:** The Star Model BM (**figure 4.6D**) is a Spanish semiautomatic pistol in the style of a Colt M1911, chambered in 9 × 19 mm Parabellum.

FIGURE 4.6. Military surplus handguns can be a way to get a well-made handgun relatively inexpensively. **A.** A Russian TT-33 chambered in 7.62 × 25 mm Tokarev. **B.** A Czechoslovakian CZ 52 chambered in 7.62 × 25 mm Tokarev. **C.** A Czechoslovakian CZ 82 chambered in 9 × 18 mm Makarov. **D.** A Spanish Star Model BM chambered in 9 × 19 mm Parabellum.

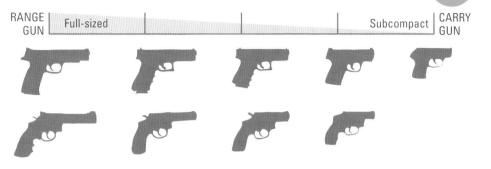

FIGURE 4.5. Every handgun on the market today falls somewhere into a continuum between a dedicated range gun and a dedicated carry gun. Larger guns with long barrels fit at one end of the spectrum, solidly identifying as range guns. Small guns with short barrels occupy the other end of the spectrum. Handguns that fall in between are attempting to merge aspects of both categories.

Taking advice from friends as to what to buy might not always be the best policy, particularly if they are casual shooters. People have a tendency to recommend what they own as a means to justify their own purchases, even if these might have been a mistake. A good example of this is when someone insists that you buy a carry gun that shoots .40 S & W because it is a more powerful round than the 9 × 19 mm Parabellum, which many people favor for concealed carry. The .40 S & W is more powerful, but it is much less pleasant to shoot and could easily deter someone from shooting. This will be touched on more completely in the next section.

4.2.4. Carrying a Handgun for Defense

Deciding to carry a handgun for self-defense is a serious decision, and one not to be taken lightly. If you are carrying a gun to broadcast your power or status, you are not taking firearms seriously. Critically, you must decide whether you would be able to shoot someone if put into a situation where you might need to use your handgun. If you do not think that you could do that, you should not be carrying a gun. In a defensive situation, you will not have the time to question your morals. Every second matters, and a moment of hesitation could cost you your life.

When you are considering whether to carry a handgun, it is beneficial to be aware of how your body reacts under high-stress situations, such as one where you might be forced to defend yourself. In such a situation, your body is suddenly switching from a state of relaxation to a state of high alert.

To better understand your body's response to these situations, we need to know something about the autonomic nervous system, which controls everything in your body that you do not have conscious control over, such as your digestion, respiratory rate, and heart rate (**figure 4.7**). The autonomic nervous system is separated into two branches: the sympathetic nervous system and the parasympathetic nervous system. The sympathetic nervous system raises your heart rate, helps increase airflow to your lungs, inhibits digestion, triggers the breakdown of fat and glycogen reserves for energy, and heightens alertness. The parasympathetic nervous system does the opposite: it lowers your heart rate, relaxes your breathing rate, and increases digestion. The majority of your organs receive both sympathetic and parasympathetic signals. Despite the two systems being in opposition, both are usually active, though—depending on the situation—one system might dominate. The sympathetic nervous system dominates in cases of emergencies to mobilize energy, while the parasympathetic nervous system dominates when you are in a relaxed state (such as when you are sleeping).*

* Lauralee Sherwood, *Human Physiology: From Cells to Systems*, 9th ed. (Boston: Cengage Learning, 2015).

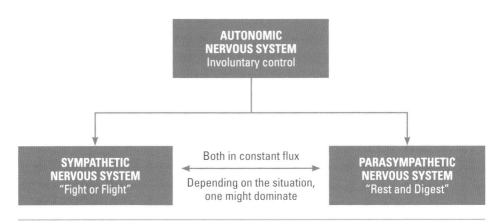

FIGURE 4.7. The autonomic nervous system is a branch of the nervous system that deals with processes that you do not have conscious control over, such as your heart rate. It is split into the sympathetic nervous system and the parasympathetic nervous system. The sympathetic nervous system is responsible for the "fight or flight" response, which is triggered by fear and extremely stressful situations, while the parasympathetic nervous system is responsible for maintaining processes such as digestion while you are in a relaxed state (sometimes called the "rest and digest" response). Normally, both systems are partially active, though in times of extreme stress, your sympathetic nervous system will dominate to help you surmount the dangerous situation.

When you are subjected to the extreme stress of having to defend yourself, your sympathetic nervous system kicks into place to mobilize your body's energy reserves to help you deal with the situation. This is commonly known as the "fight or flight" response (though it is sometimes called the fight, flight, or freeze response, as we will touch on later). The sympathetic nervous system triggers a surge in hormones such as adrenaline that lead to the aforementioned physiological changes in your body. The elevated heart rate, increased airflow to your lungs, and breakdown of energy reserves are all to make sure that your muscles are supplied with oxygenated and nutrient-filled blood to be ready for vigorous activity. While all these things are helpful for surmounting a dangerous situation, stress-induced activation of the sympathetic nervous system has some other consequences that are less helpful. You will often lose the ability to perform precise movements with your fingers (fine motor skills). Your vision will narrow to focus on the threat in front of you (tunnel vision), and you lose your peripheral vision. Your hearing can be attenuated or temporarily lost (known as auditory exclusion). The extent to which these phenomena manifest themselves depends on the intensity of the fear-induced stress.* As the levels of stress increase, so too does your heart rate. The loss of fine motor skills comes first, followed by the loss of peripheral vision and the onset of auditory exclusion. If stress levels continue to mount and your heart rate continues to rise, your actions start to

* Lt. Col. David Grossman, *On Combat: The Psychology and Physiology of Deadly Conflict in War and in Peace*, 3rd ed. (Millstadt, IL: Warrior Science Publications, 2008).

become less controllable. It is at these high stress levels that you might irrationally flee or even freeze and be unable to do anything (hence, fight, flight, or freeze). Not everyone responds to these situations of extreme stress in the same way, so you cannot predict exactly how you would respond if put in one. However, it is important to be aware of what can and often does happen in these situations, so that you are prepared for them.

You need to be aware of the physiological effects of the sympathetic nervous system and train for them if you want to respond effectively in a defensive situation. Your heart will be racing, and it will be difficult to disengage the safety on your handgun with your deteriorating fine motor skills, particularly if you have not practiced it extensively. If your handgun is not loaded, you will fumble with inserting the magazine. If your handgun does not have a round in the chamber, you might struggle pulling back the slide and chambering a round.

Time is never a luxury in a life-or-death situation. You might not have the time to pull back the slide on your handgun to chamber a round. You might have time to turn off the safety, but if you have not practiced it enough for it to be muscle memory, you will likely struggle with it. Glock handguns do not have any manual/active safeties, and while that might seem odd at first, it makes perfect sense for a self-defense gun or something for active duty. They are designed with defensive situations in mind, knowing that the gun needs to be ready the moment it is drawn from a holster. Remember, the only thing that makes a firearm safe is its user.

4.2.4.1. What Handgun Should You Get for Concealed Carry?

The ideal handgun for concealed carry is going to be different for everyone. But to make a general rule, the best carry gun is the one that you are willing to consistently carry. If you have a gun but do not always carry it, it does not do you any good. A larger handgun might be easy for you to shoot well, but if you will not consistently carry it because of its weight, it is not a good defensive gun.

Aside from the size of the gun, there is a lot of discussion concerning the best cartridge for a carry gun. The .380 ACP (9 × 17 mm) is common in a lot of smaller carry guns, though many shooters claim that it is not powerful enough to stop a threat. The 9 × 19 mm Parabellum is very popular in carry guns; it has a 9 mm caliber bullet like the .380 ACP, but a larger case affording additional gunpowder, and, as such, it is more powerful. Despite this, there are still those who say that you need a larger-caliber cartridge such as a .40 S & W or .45 ACP to effectively stop a threat. These cartridges have larger bullets that can often incapacitate a person in fewer shots, but it can be harder to effectively control the recoil, especially in a small handgun designed for concealment. Much like with the size of a gun, the best cartridge to use for concealed carry is the one that you will consistently carry. Some calibers might be more powerful, but if that extra power makes the gun unpleasant to shoot, you might be disinclined to carry it.

Once you have found a gun to conceal, your challenges are not over. You still need to find an effective and comfortable means to carry it, and that can be as difficult as finding the right firearm. The most common way to carry a handgun is with a holster attached to your belt. They usually come in two permutations: outside the waistband (**figure 4.8A**) and inside the waistband (**figure 4.8B**). With an outside-the-waistband holster, the holster attaches to your belt and lies completely outside your pants. An inside-the-waistband holster still attaches to your belt, but it is put on the inside of your pants. Inside-the-waistband holsters often make concealing a firearm easier, but they are less comfortable than outside-the-waistband holsters and often require that you buy pants slightly larger than normal to accommodate the size of the gun.

FIGURE 4.8. After finding a handgun to conceal, you have to decide how best to conceal it. **A.** An outside-the-waistband holster stays completely outside your pants. The extra bulk can make the handgun hard to conceal unless you are wearing a jacket. **B.** An inside-the-waistband holster attaches to your belt and tucks inside the waistband of your pants. This makes the handgun easier to conceal but is usually less comfortable.

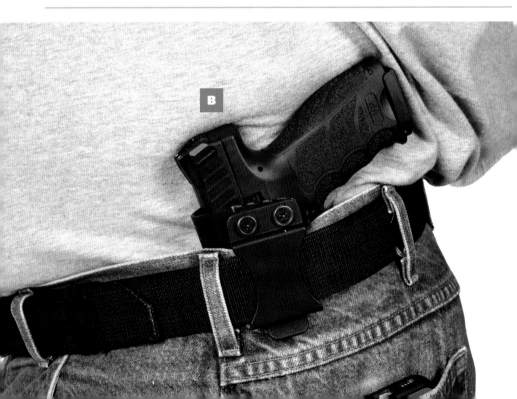

4.2.5. Should You Use a Laser Sight?

Anyone who has seen an action movie in the last twenty years or so will likely be familiar with using lasers to aim firearms. What started out as a staple of science fiction is now rooted in practical and readily available technology. Laser sights have made considerable advancements in recent years, becoming smaller and more reliable. Laser sights come in numerous different forms, including those built into the frame of the handgun (**figure 4.9A**), those attached to the trigger guard (**figure 4.9B**), and those built into the handle (**figure 4.9C**). But, is a laser sight something that you would want to consider for a defensive handgun or for a range gun?

Laser sights can be helpful for someone learning how to shoot. They make it easy to determine where your natural point of aim (see section 4.1.3) is located. Also, they can help you determine whether you are moving your gun when you press the trigger (as discussed further in section 5.2.2, if you impart additional movement to the handgun while pressing the trigger, you will not hit the target where you intend). Beyond training, laser sights have uses in defensive situations. A laser can serve as a good deterrent, since most people would think twice about their actions if a laser were shining on their chest. Also, in a defensive situation, you might be forced to shoot from an unconventional position, one that you have not practiced shooting from. In such an instance, a laser can help ensure that you hit your target.

Laser sights are not without downsides, however. Their main fault is that they add an extra layer of complexity and another instance for things to fail. They provide an opening for Murphy's law, the adage stating that "anything that can go wrong, will go wrong." Laser sights run on batteries, which do not retain a charge indefinitely. You do not want your laser to fail the moment that you need it. Because of this, it is imperative that you also practice with your iron sights, even if you have a laser sight. Another potential problem is that red lasers can be difficult to see in full daylight. Laser sights come both in red and green. Green lasers are easier for the human eye to see than red, and they are visible in direct sunlight. Green lasers are also more expensive than red lasers, since the technology for green lasers is newer.

FIGURE 4.9. Laser sights are available in many different permutations. **A.** Some laser sights are built directly into the frame of the handgun, like with this Smith & Wesson Bodyguard. This laser sight can be activated by pressing the red button above the trigger guard. **B.** Other laser sights can be attached to the trigger guard of the handgun, like with this Glock 42. The red button on the laser sight will activate it when pressed. **C.** Still other laser sights are built into the handle of the firearm, like with this Smith & Wesson Airweight Revolver. In this instance, holding the revolver properly will press a button on the handle, activating the laser.

SHOOTING
A HANDGUN

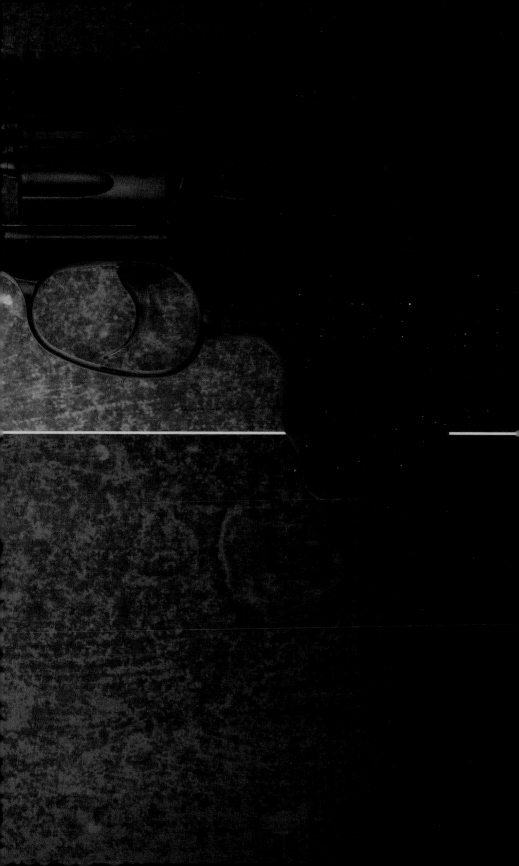

CHAPTER 5 SHOOTING A HANDGUN

The process of shooting a handgun is a fairly simple one. You need to present the pistol with a consistent grip and stance, acquire the correct sight picture while aiming, and press the trigger without moving the gun. In the simplest sense, shooting a firearm effectively can be broken into two tenets: (1) present the pistol consistently and then (2) do not move the gun when pressing the trigger. These are straightforward concepts to understand, but a lot of different things go into effectively implementing them. In this chapter, these two tenets will be discussed in detail, breaking each into three fundamentals.

The first tenet, being able to present the pistol consistently, is achievable by understanding and implementing these three fundamentals:

1. grip

2. stance and firearm presentation

3. sight alignment and sight picture

The second tenet, not moving the gun when pressing the trigger, is achievable by understanding and implementing these three fundamentals:

1. breath control

2. trigger control

3. follow-through

Each of these fundamentals will be discussed in detail in this chapter, the first tenet in section 5.1 and the second tenet in section 5.2. If you have never shot before, it is often easier to pick up the fundamentals than for those who have shot, since you have not had the opportunity to develop bad habits. Additionally, there are a few other tips for improving your shooting that are discussed in section 5.3.

5.1. Presenting the Handgun Consistently

The first tenet of shooting effectively is learning how to be consistent. If you hold the handgun differently every time that you pick it up, you cannot expect to hit the same place on the target with each shot. Mastering how you hold the firearm, or how you "grip" it, is the first fundamental toward achieving consistency. Additionally, if you change the position of your body and how you hold yourself with every shot, you will not consistently hit the same place. Deciding on an effective stance is the second fundamental toward being able to consistently present a handgun. Finally, if you align the handgun sights on the target differently with every shot, you cannot expect a consistent shot placement. Sight alignment and sight picture is the third fundamental for consistency.

In this section, these three aspects will be discussed in detail: grip in section 5.1.1, stance and firearm presentation in section 5.1.2, and sight alignment and sight picture in section 5.1.3.

5.1.1. Grip

How you hold a handgun is colloquially known as how you "grip" the firearm. It describes how you situate your fingers around the handle of the gun, such that your index finger can easily reach the trigger. Your grip is your direct interface with the firearm, so it is fairly self-evident that it plays an important role in how effectively you shoot it.

Having a consistent hand placement is extremely important if you want to reliably hit a target. If you are holding the handgun differently every time you shoot it, this variability will translate into an inconsistent placement of shots on the target. Because of this, it is essential to have a defined place for all of your fingers on the handle of the gun, including your thumb. Most handguns are designed with the right-handed shooter in mind but can be easily fired with your left hand.

What distinguishes a handgun from other firearms is that it can be operated single-handedly. The initial focus in this section will be on holding a handgun single-handedly, before discussing how to hold it with two hands.

5.1.1.1. Right-Handed Grip

The web between your thumb and index finger should be as high as possible on the backstrap of the handgun's grip (**figure 5.1A**). The higher your grasp is, the better control you have over the recoil of the firearm. It allows the recoil of the firearm to be transferred horizontally into your arm. If your grip is too low, the recoil will cause the muzzle to rock up and backward in your hand, with your hand acting almost like the pivot/fulcrum of a lever (**figure 5.1B**). There are two possibilities for the placement of your thumb: (1) resting it on your middle finger to add support (**figure 5.1B**), or (2) having it point forward in the direction of the target (**figure 5.1C**). Either of these positions is effective, and it largely comes down to what feels most comfortable. You should rest your index/shooting finger on the frame of the firearm, straight and extended (**figure 5.1D, E**). It should never be on the trigger unless you are ready to shoot, nor should it be on or within the trigger guard. It is helpful to find a place on the frame to index your finger, such that you can become accustomed to placing your finger at that same place every time that you grip the handgun. Your middle finger should rest against the bottom of the trigger guard of the handgun (**figure 5.1B, C, D**). With your thumb, index finger, and middle finger properly in position, your other two fingers should fall into place on the grip. With smaller handguns, it might be necessary to place your pinky finger underneath the bottom of the handle (**figure 5.1F**). This grip works equally well both

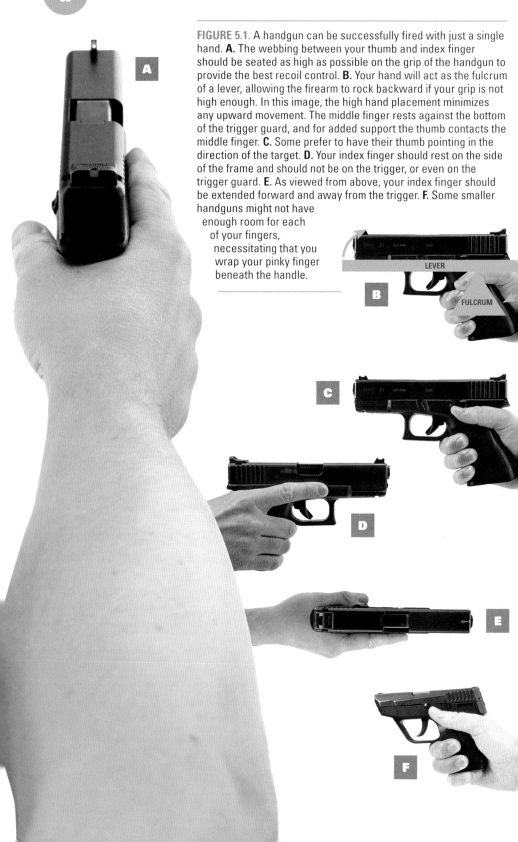

FIGURE 5.1. A handgun can be successfully fired with just a single hand. **A.** The webbing between your thumb and index finger should be seated as high as possible on the grip of the handgun to provide the best recoil control. **B.** Your hand will act as the fulcrum of a lever, allowing the firearm to rock backward if your grip is not high enough. In this image, the high hand placement minimizes any upward movement. The middle finger rests against the bottom of the trigger guard, and for added support the thumb contacts the middle finger. **C.** Some prefer to have their thumb pointing in the direction of the target. **D.** Your index finger should rest on the side of the frame and should not be on the trigger, or even on the trigger guard. **E.** As viewed from above, your index finger should be extended forward and away from the trigger. **F.** Some smaller handguns might not have enough room for each of your fingers, necessitating that you wrap your pinky finger beneath the handle.

LEVER

FULCRUM

for semiautomatic handguns and revolvers (**figure 5.2A, B**). It positions your thumb to access the controls of most handguns, such as the safety, slide stop, and magazine release. Sometimes these features will be ambidextrous, but if not, they are nearly always situated for the right hand. Revolvers do not have slide stops or magazine releases, but many have cylinder releases, which are traditionally on the left side (**figure 5.2C**).

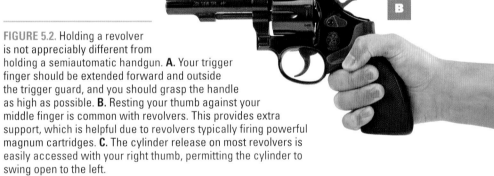

FIGURE 5.2. Holding a revolver is not appreciably different from holding a semiautomatic handgun. **A.** Your trigger finger should be extended forward and outside the trigger guard, and you should grasp the handle as high as possible. **B.** Resting your thumb against your middle finger is common with revolvers. This provides extra support, which is helpful due to revolvers typically firing powerful magnum cartridges. **C.** The cylinder release on most revolvers is easily accessed with your right thumb, permitting the cylinder to swing open to the left.

Slide stop

FIGURE 5.3. Nearly every semiautomatic pistol has a slide stop to hold the slide back after shooting the final cartridge in the magazine. **A.** Pictured is a Glock 19, with the slide stop indicated. **B.** Pictured is a Glock 19 pistol with its slide in the back position, anchored by the slide stop.

Slide stop

The Israeli Grip

In Israel, all members of the military are taught to shoot with the right hand, regardless of their dominant hand. They stress that a handgun is not called a handsgun, meaning that it was designed to be fired with a single hand. In a combat situation, the likelihood of needing your other hand to do something else is high. The grip position they recommend is very similar to the one described above, though they always position the thumb to touch the tip of the middle finger (**figure 5.4A**). This provides the greatest amount of support to the weapon if you are holding it with only one hand. For shooting with two hands, position your left hand such that the left thumb seats on top of the right thumb (**figure 5.4B**). This position ensures that neither thumb will interact with any of the controls unintentionally. Shooting with both hands will be discussed in greater detail later in this section.

FIGURE 5.4. The Israeli military teaches everyone to shoot with their right hand, regardless of their dominant hand. **A.** When holding the handgun with a single hand, your thumb should contact your middle finger to maximize support. **B.** When shooting with two hands, the thumb of your nonshooting hand should cover the thumb of your shooting hand.

5.1.1.2. Left-Handed Grip

The majority of the information about gripping a handgun with your right hand also applies to the left hand. You still want to keep the web between your index finger and thumb as high as possible on the gun and keep your index finger away from the trigger. With semiautomatic handguns, the slide stop, safety, and magazine release are generally on the left side of the slide (**figure 5.5A**), and your index finger will often be lying over the top of them or against them (**figure 5.5B**). This can be uncomfortable and irritating if any of these parts are pronounced. Besides the discomfort, they can be more difficult to use. This is particularly the case with the slide stop, which, due to its proximity to the slide, will always be in contact with the user's trigger finger. Because of this, using the slide stop to release the slide is difficult, necessitating that the user becomes accustomed to manually pulling back the slide.

With nearly all double-action revolvers, the cylinder opens to the left (**figure 5.5C**). This makes loading easy for a right-handed individual, since the cylinder is in easy reach of your unoccupied left hand. If you are holding the revolver in your left hand, the cylinder opens away from you and into your trigger finger (**figure 5.5D**). This often necessitates transferring the revolver to your other hand to facilitate loading.

FIGURE 5.5. Shooting left-handed adds some additional complications since most handguns were designed for right-handed shooters. **A.** The slide stop on a semiautomatic handgun is universally on the left side and is very hard to use if you are shooting left-handed. **B.** When shooting left-handed, your trigger finger will obscure the slide stop and could be irritated by other controls, such as the magazine release or safety. **C.** The cylinder of most revolvers opens to the left, which facilitates easy loading for a right-handed shooter. **D.** If you are shooting left-handed, the cylinder opens into your trigger finger, making loading more difficult.

5.1.1.3. Forearm Position

Outside of thumb and finger placement when gripping a firearm, it is important to be mindful of the firearm's relationship to your shooting arm. Your forearm should be in line with the firearm (**figure 5.6A**), allowing the recoil to be absorbed by your arm. If the handgun is not aligned with your forearm (**figure 5.6B**), the recoil of the gun is largely absorbed by your thumb. This can be painful, and it does not allow you to properly control the

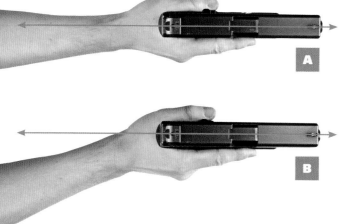

FIGURE 5.6. When shooting single-handedly, the firearm should line up with the forearm of your shooting hand. **A.** You should be able to draw a straight line from your handgun to your forearm. **B.** If the firearm is not aligned with your forearm, the recoil will largely be absorbed by your thumb.

firearm, requiring you to spend more time reacquiring the target after each shot. This commonly happens if the grip of a handgun is too large for your hand, and you compensate by altering your grip to properly reach the trigger.

5.1.1.4. Consistency

One of the main strengths of this style of holding a handgun is that it is easy to do it consistently. If you want your shots to continually hit the same area on a target, you need your grip to be consistent. Every time you pick up a handgun, you should use it as an opportunity to train holding it properly. If you are not able to replicate the grip described here because of severe arthritis, or because you are missing a digit on your shooting hand, it can be modified into something that you are capable of doing, and something that you can do consistently. It is important to note that you should always obtain the proper grip with your dominant hand first before trying to add your second hand, which will be discussed below.

5.1.1.5. Two-Handed Grip

While a handgun can be fired effectively with a single hand, most shooters prefer a two-handed grip because of the additional control and recoil absorption it provides. For a two-handed grip, your shooting hand should be kept in the position described earlier, but your nondominant hand can adopt a number of different positions. There is not one correct position for your second hand, but there is one that is easiest to do consistently.

Recommended Positioning of Nondominant Hand

For the recommended position, take your nondominant hand and position it like you are about to shake someone's hand (**figure 5.7A**). Cock your hand downward, as if you are going into a handshake (**figure 5.7B**). This may be slightly awkward if your nondominant hand is your left hand and you are unaccustomed to using that hand for a handshake. With your hand in this cocked position, it is now perfectly suited to lock in beside your other hand around the gun. Depending on the positioning of your thumb on your shooting hand, your nondominant thumb will differ. If your shooting thumb is bent and touching your middle finger (**figure 5.1B**), your second thumb should be positioned over the top of the first (**figure 5.7C, D**). However, if your shooting thumb is pointing forward and not contacting your middle finger, it is often more comfortable to position the second thumb below the first and point it forward in the direction of the target (**figure 5.7E, F, G**). It should be noted that the placement of your thumb when shooting single-handedly does not have to dictate what two-handed grip you adopt. It is completely acceptable to shoot single-handedly with your thumb contacting your middle finger, but then to move that thumb when you adopt the two-handed grip, such that you can have both thumbs pointing forward. Regardless, either permutation of this two-handed grip gives you a very good balance. It allows you to push forward with the shooting hand and pull backward with the other; this equal/isometric action helps keep the gun in place. Isometric action can also be supplied laterally by pressing your hands together. It is important to note that when using this grip with a revolver, you should make sure that neither of your thumbs extend beyond the cylinder, since hot gas is released from that point when the gun is fired (**figure 5.7H**).

FIGURE 5.7. A double-handed grip is the ideal way to shoot a handgun, since it provides extra support and stability. **A.** Position your nondominant hand as if you are going to shake someone's hand, and (**B**) cock your hand downward as you would if you were going into the shake. Your hand is now in the position to wrap around the fingers of your dominant hand. **C, D.** Your index finger of your nondominant hand should rest against the trigger guard, and your other fingers should follow suit, wrapping around the fingers of your shooting hand. The thumb of your nondominant hand should cover the thumb of your shooting hand. This positioning works equally well for semiautomatics and revolvers. **E.** If the thumb of your shooting hand is pointing toward your target, the thumb of your nondominant hand can slide below it, also pointing toward the target. Your index finger should rest below the trigger guard, and the other fingers will fall into place. **F.** A downward view of the two-handed grip with both thumbs pointing in the direction of the target. **G.** The two-handed grip with both thumbs pointing forward works equally well for revolvers. **H.** When holding a revolver with two hands, make sure that neither of your thumbs extend past the cylinder, since hot gas is released when firing. The pictured positioning is incorrect and will result in a burned thumb.

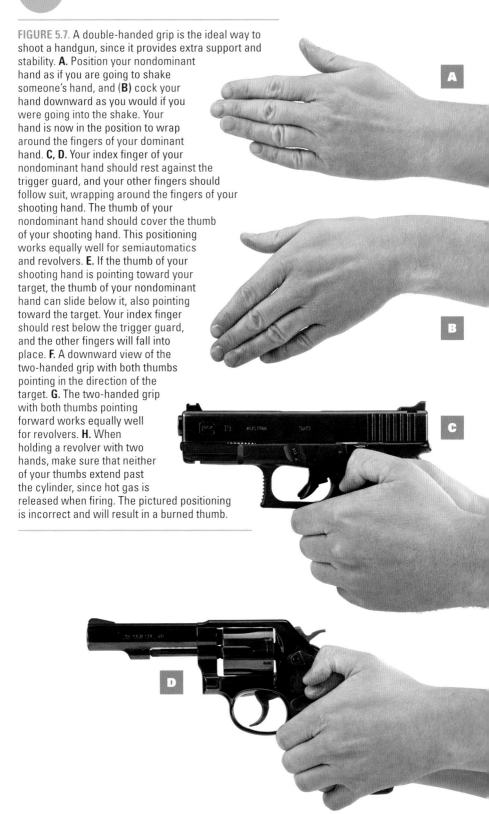

Teacup position

The teacup position should be recognizable to anyone who has seen action films or police dramas on television. To implement it, you wrap your nondominant hand around the base of the handgun, creating a "cup" (**figure 5.8A, B**). With this position, your shooting hand has to do all of the stabilizing, since the cupped hand is not in a position to add any sort of stabilizing pressure. There is nothing inherently wrong about using the teacup position, but it is hard to consistently keep the firearm steady when using it, and the first tenet of shooting effectively is being consistent.

FIGURE 5.8. There are a number of common two-handed grips that are not recommended, because your second hand does not add any support to the firearm. **A, B.** In the teacup position, your nonshooting hand is placed at the base of the grip, cupping the bottom of your shooting hand. **C.** Clasping your second hand around the wrist of your shooting hand does not add any support or provide any noticeable benefit.

Hand around wrist position

Sometimes, people will wrap their nondominant hand around the wrist of their shooting hand, as if to support it (**figure 5.8C**). This grip does not do anything to help support the gun. Like the teacup position, this one is not inherently wrong, but you might as well just shoot single-handedly, since your second hand is not adding any support to the firearm.

Incorrect positions

One of the worst grips is to place the thumb of your nondominant hand behind the slide (**figure 5.9**). This positioning is not advisable because the slide will hit your thumb as it moves backward, tearing your skin and making a bad first impression for new shooters.

FIGURE 5.9. Having an improper grip on your handgun will not only lead to inconsistent shot placement but can also hurt you. Wrapping the thumb of your nonshooting hand behind the slide is dangerous, since the slide moves backward with every shot.

5.1.2. Stance and Firearm Presentation

The second important element to presenting a firearm consistently is your arm and body positioning, also referred to as your "stance." Your stance should provide you with a strong and stable platform to base your shooting around. There are two main schools of thought pertaining to basic stances for shooting handguns: the Weaver stance and the isosceles stance. Each of these stances has its own strengths and weaknesses and has practical uses depending on the situation. It is helpful to be familiar with and practice each stance, since you never know what position you will be able to adopt if you need to defend yourself. In a defensive situation, it is unlikely that you will have sufficient time to get into your preferred stance.

5.1.2.1. Weaver

The Weaver stance is one of the most recognizable two-handed shooting stances. It is named after its innovator, Los Angeles County deputy sheriff Jack Weaver, who designed it as a means to

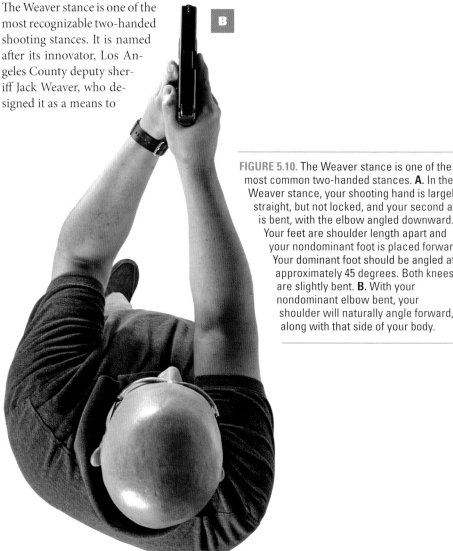

FIGURE 5.10. The Weaver stance is one of the most common two-handed stances. **A.** In the Weaver stance, your shooting hand is largely straight, but not locked, and your second arm is bent, with the elbow angled downward. Your feet are shoulder length apart and your nondominant foot is placed forward. Your dominant foot should be angled at approximately 45 degrees. Both knees are slightly bent. **B.** With your nondominant elbow bent, your shoulder will naturally angle forward, along with that side of your body.

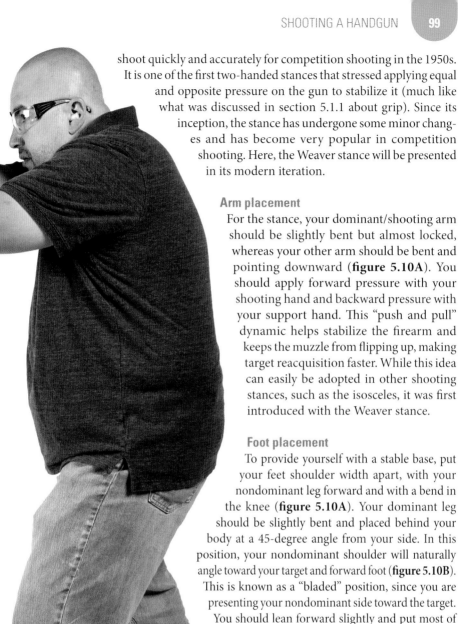

shoot quickly and accurately for competition shooting in the 1950s. It is one of the first two-handed stances that stressed applying equal and opposite pressure on the gun to stabilize it (much like what was discussed in section 5.1.1 about grip). Since its inception, the stance has undergone some minor changes and has become very popular in competition shooting. Here, the Weaver stance will be presented in its modern iteration.

Arm placement

For the stance, your dominant/shooting arm should be slightly bent but almost locked, whereas your other arm should be bent and pointing downward (**figure 5.10A**). You should apply forward pressure with your shooting hand and backward pressure with your support hand. This "push and pull" dynamic helps stabilize the firearm and keeps the muzzle from flipping up, making target reacquisition faster. While this idea can easily be adopted in other shooting stances, such as the isosceles, it was first introduced with the Weaver stance.

Foot placement

To provide yourself with a stable base, put your feet shoulder width apart, with your nondominant leg forward and with a bend in the knee (**figure 5.10A**). Your dominant leg should be slightly bent and placed behind your body at a 45-degree angle from your side. In this position, your nondominant shoulder will naturally angle toward your target and forward foot (**figure 5.10B**). This is known as a "bladed" position, since you are presenting your nondominant side toward the target. You should lean forward slightly and put most of your weight on your front foot. This foot placement is common in martial arts and is known as a boxing stance. The relative closeness of your feet allows for rapid position changes and pivoting, and the forward lean provides ample stability from being pushed backward. This narrowness of the stance does not provide much side-to-side stability, however.

A

FIGURE 5.11. The isosceles stance is easy to adopt consistently. **A.** In the isosceles stance, both arms are straight and locked at the elbows. Your feet are shoulder length apart and aligned, with a slight bend at the knees. **B.** With both arms straight, your arms form an isosceles triangle, which is how the stance's name was derived.

B

5.1.2.2. Isosceles

The isosceles stance is the other prominent shooting stance, and the one that is easiest to adopt consistently.

Arm placement

As with the Weaver stance, the isosceles is a two-handed stance, but unlike the Weaver, you extend both arms fully forward (**figure 5.11A**). Your body and shoulders should be squared with the target. Viewed from above, your arms and chest placement should form an isosceles triangle (**figure 5.11B**); hence the stance's name. The "push and pull" dynamic from the Weaver stance can, and should, be applied to the isosceles stance. However, due to both arms being straight, it is impossible to have the firearm perfectly align with the forearm of your shooting hand (as discussed in section 5.1.1). Because of this, the recoil is distributed equally between both arms, as opposed to just the forearm of your shooting hand.

Foot placement

To create a stable base for shooting, your feet should be shoulder length apart and lined up with your body (**figure 5.11A**). You should bend your legs at your knees and lean your body forward. This stance is very stable from side to side, but, due to the alignment of the feet, it is not as stable front to back. The positioning of your feet can affect shot placement on the target. Oftentimes, if you are shooting right-handed, just moving your right foot back a few inches can result in pulling your shots to the right side of the target. This is not a hard and fast rule, however. If your shots are consistently being pulled to one side of the target, small changes in your foot placement can lead to noticeable changes on the target. Additionally, experimenting with your foot placement can help you determine your natural aiming position.

5.1.2.3. Ready Position

You will not always be in a situation where it is appropriate to be in your shooting stance with your handgun up. However, you may be anticipating using it shortly, so you need your handgun in a position that can be easily transformed into a shooting position. You want your gun to be in a "ready" position. There are numerous ready positions, depending on the situation, though this book will cover only a single position, the "low ready" position.

Low ready position

When at the shooting range or at a competitive shooting event, the easiest ready position to adopt

FIGURE 5.12. The low ready position is ideal for on the range, when you are getting ready to shoot. **A.** If you are at an outdoor shooting range, you should have the handgun lowered to the ground at a 45-degree angle. **B**. When shooting at an indoor range, you should keep the firearm pointed down range, but keep the gun parallel to the ground.

is known as the low ready position. It is a modification of your shooting stance, where you do not have your arms extended, but the firearm is still pointed down range (**figure 5.12**). Depending on where you are shooting, the exact positioning of the firearm will differ. If you are at an outdoor shooting range, you should have the gun pointed at a 45-degree angle to the ground (**figure 5.12A**). If the firearm were accidentally discharged, the bullet would strike the ground safely. If you are at an indoor range, you do not want the firearm pointing at the ground, since a discharged round could ricochet off the floor. Because of this, you should have the gun pointed down range, parallel to the ground (**figure 5.12B**). With both of these variations, your foot and shoulder positions are modeled off the shooting stance that you are using (Weaver or isosceles). You still should have a proper grip on the handgun. Since your feet are in the proper position and you have an effective grip on the firearm, all you have to do is bring the gun up to your eyes to shoot. There is an important point here that deserves emphasis: When you bring the gun up, you should always move the gun to meet your eyes. You do not want to move your head and eyes to find the firearm.

The low ready position works best in areas that are not crowded with people moving around you. While it is always essential to be aware of your surroundings, when in the low ready position, you need to be distinctly aware of anyone who could walk into your field of view, since the firearm is extended in front of you.

5.1.3. Sight Alignment and Sight Picture

The final element required to consistently present your firearm is learning how to align the sights properly. Knowing how to properly align the front sight between the sides of the notch of the rear sight is an important component of aiming (referred to as sight alignment). Furthermore, the relationship between the sights and the target (referred to as sight picture) bears equal weight. Learning these two things is one of the most critical aspects of learning how to shoot effectively. Even if you have a perfect grip on your handgun and an excellent stance, if you are not properly aligning your sights, you will not hit where you intend (though you might consistently hit that unintended area). Before talking specifically about sight alignment and sight picture, it is important to address a related topic that influences it: eye dominance.

5.1.3.1. Eye Dominance

When processing visual inputs received from your eyes, your brain prefers inputs from one eye. This phenomenon is known as ocular dominance, or eye dominance. This "dominant" eye is the one that your brain largely uses to determine the positioning of objects. Oftentimes, an individual's dominant eye will match their dominant hand, such that a right-handed individual is frequently right-eye dominant, though this is not always the case.

When shooting a firearm, you generally want to align the sights with your dominant eye, since it does the best job of properly positioning the target. This is particularly true when shooting a rifle, since the firearm is brought up to your shoulder, close to your shooting eye. Customarily, the shooter will close their other eye, focusing solely on the one brought up to the rifle's sights. If you are primarily aiming through your nondominant eye, you might find it hard to properly align the sights with your target. This is less critical when shooting a handgun, since you are holding the firearm at arm's length, and the sights are not up close to a particular eye. Ideally, you should be shooting your handgun with both eyes open, so you will not be relying on a single eye for target acquisition and sight alignment.

A simple method known as the Porta test was designed to determine your dominant eye, by the Italian scholar Giambattista della Porta back in 1593.* For this test, extend one of your arms out in front of your body and use your thumb to cover a distant object, such as the center of a target or a light switch (**figure 5.13**). Focus on your thumb with both eyes open and then close your left eye. Take note of where the object is in relationship to your thumb. Now, open your left eye and close your right eye, and take note of where the object is located. In most cases, when you close one of your eyes, the object will appear to move to the left or right of your thumb. The open eye that does not experience a shift is your dominant eye. Most people have a dominant eye that matches with their dominant hand, but this is not always the case. Some individuals are cross-dominant, where their dominant eye is at odds with their dominant hand.

* Heidi L. Roth, Andrea N. Lora, and Kenneth M. Heilman, "Effects of Monocular Viewing and Eye Dominance on Spatial Attention," *Brain* 125, no. 9 (2002): 2023–2035.

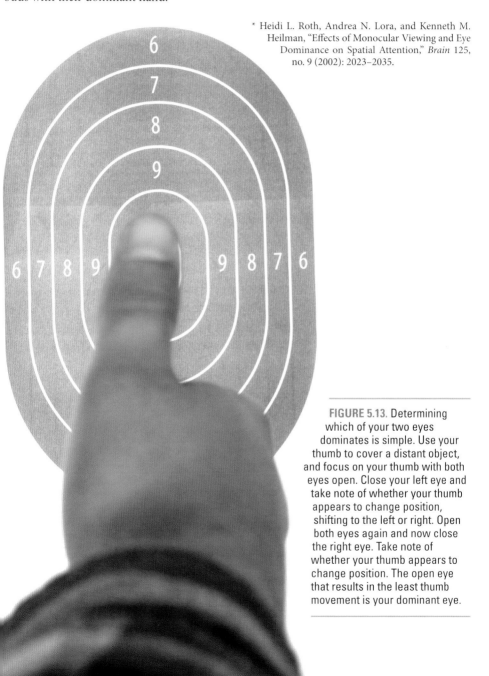

FIGURE 5.13. Determining which of your two eyes dominates is simple. Use your thumb to cover a distant object, and focus on your thumb with both eyes open. Close your left eye and take note of whether your thumb appears to change position, shifting to the left or right. Open both eyes again and now close the right eye. Take note of whether your thumb appears to change position. The open eye that results in the least thumb movement is your dominant eye.

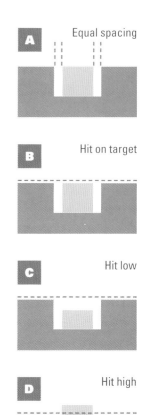

FIGURE 5.14. Sight alignment. **A.** The front sight should be between the two sides of the notch of the rear sight, with equal spacing on either side. **B.** The top edge of the front and rear sights should be aligned to hit the target where you intend. **C.** If the front sight is buried within the notch of the rear sight, your shots will hit the target lower than you intend. **D.** If the front sight is raised above the notch of the rear sight, your shots will hit the target higher than you intend.

When shooting a handgun, it is best to keep both eyes open. This puts less strain on the eyes and provides better depth perception and better peripheral vision. If you get into a habit of closing one of your eyes and do not realize that you are cross-dominant, you will likely be closing your dominant eye, which will significantly affect your performance. If you find that you cannot initially shoot with both eyes open, make sure that you determine which eye is your dominant eye, and keep that one open. Learning to shoot with both eyes open is something that can be developed with time and practice.

5.1.3.2. Sight Alignment

Sight alignment is the relationship between the front sight and the rear sight. The vast majority of pistols have a post as a front sight and a notched rear sight. With this setup, the front post should be centered within the notch of the rear sight, with an equal distance on either side (**figure 5.14A**). The top of each of the sights should be aligned (**figure 5.14B**). Burying the front sight in the notch will result in you shooting low (**figure 5.14C**), whereas raising the front sight above the notch will result in your shots going high (**figure 5.14D**), which is a common issue with short-barreled revolvers (commonly called snub-nosed revolvers) due to their minimal rear sights.

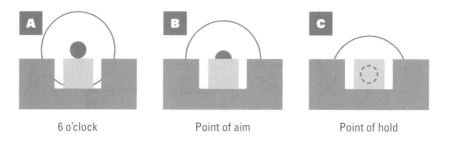

6 o'clock   Point of aim   Point of hold

FIGURE 5.15. Sight alignment. **A.** For the 6 o'clock position, position the point that you want to hit on top of the front sight. **B.** For the point-of-aim position, you bisect what you want to hit with the top of your front sight. **C.** For the point-of-hold position, center the front site over the top of what you want to hit.

5.1.3.3. Sight Picture

Once you have your sights properly aligned, you need to determine how those sights are oriented in relation to the target. This notion is known as sight picture. There is not one sight picture that will work perfectly for every firearm. Most manufacturers do not specify the sight picture of a firearm. The best way to determine a firearm's sight picture is to shoot the gun and try out different options until you determine the one that is most successful for you. Different shooters can shoot the same gun with different sight pictures and still be successful. It is important to find what works best for you.

One of the most common sight pictures is the 6 o'clock position (**figure 5.15A**), where you situate what you want to hit directly on top of the post of the front sight. With the "point of aim" position, you bisect what you want to hit with the front sight (**figure 5.15B**). The last common sight picture is known as "point of hold," where you cover what you want to hit with the center of the front sight (**figure 5.15C**).

5.1.3.4. Focus

After aligning your sights properly and figuring out a sight picture, you need to decide what to focus your attention on, since you cannot focus on the target, front sight, and rear sight all at the same time. It is most effective to focus specifically on the front sight. Focusing on the front sight will cause the rear sight and the target to blur slightly, but not so much as to prevent proper alignment and sight picture. The rear sight can be likened to a window. You do not focus on the windows and the curtains, you look through the window, with it framing your view outside. In the same way, the rear sight is just something to look through, something to frame the front sight that you are focusing on.

5.1.3.5. Raising the Gun to Your Eyes

Along with properly aligning the sights and orienting them with the target, you need to be cognizant of how you bring the gun into your point of view. When you raise the handgun to shoot, you want to bring it up to your eyes, such that you have to do minimal head or eye movement to find the sights. The more you have to move your head and eyes, the more time it takes for target acquisition. This goes hand in hand with your natural point of aim (see section 4.1.3), which is the position that you naturally adopt when raising the gun. If you constantly have to move your head and eyes to find your handgun's sights after raising it, you may have to make some modifications to your shooting stance to see if it improves.

5.1.3.6. Sight Enhancements

The general design of handgun sights is fairly consistent, featuring a front post and a notched rear sight, but on top of that standard design, there are numerous modifications/enhancements. One of the most common enhancements is adding a white dot on the front sight to help you specifically focus on it (**figure 5.16A**). Sometimes white dots are added on either side of the rear sight

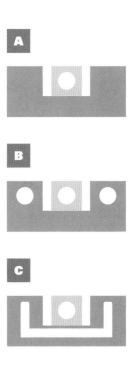

FIGURE 5.16. Sight enhancements. **A.** A white dot on the front sight makes it easier to focus on the front sight. **B.** White dots on the rear sight help align the sights by just lining up the dots. **C.** Glock handguns have a white band on the rear sight.

(**figure 5.16B**), such that sight alignment is as simple as aligning the three white dots. Glock handguns have a white band that traces around the rear sight (**figure 5.16C**). Presumably this is to aid in quickly aligning the sights, but with the predominance of white, it can make focusing on the front sight more difficult.

Fiber optic front sights are also very popular. With fiber optics, the front sight is drilled out and a piece of translucent colored plastic material (a pipe) is inserted. The colored plastic picks up light and is very easy to focus on. Fiber optic sights make sight alignment extremely rapid.

Night sights are another common sight choice, especially for those buying a defensive handgun. These sights have tritium, a radioactive isotope of hydrogen, applied to the white dots on the sight posts. This allows the dots to glow green in the dark, allowing you to properly align your sights in low-light settings. These sights do have a life span, since the half-life of tritium is around twelve years, meaning that their intensity will decrease by half after twelve years. It should be noted that if you are shooting with a flashlight, your night sights will appear as black posts.

The sights that you choose for your firearm are a matter of personal preference. There is not one type of sight that is the best in every situation. As a rule of thumb, however, plain black sights are generally considered to be the most accurate sights, but they take longer to acquire a sight picture.

5.2. Do Not Move the Gun When Pressing the Trigger

Once you are able to consistently present your handgun, you need to be able to press the trigger without imparting movement on the gun. A perfect grip and stance will be spoiled if you jerk the entirety of the gun as you are pressing the trigger. There are three aspects that play into pressing the trigger without moving the gun: breath control, trigger control, and follow-through.

In this section, these three aspects will be discussed in detail: breath control in section 5.2.1, trigger control in section 5.2.2, and follow-through in section 5.2.3.

5.2.1. Breath Control

The process of breathing results in a rise and fall of your chest and shoulders. This movement is transferred to your arms, which affects your sight alignment and sight picture. Because of this, it is important to consider your breathing while shooting. Breath control is the process of learning to reduce the amount of handgun movement associated with your breathing.

When shooting for leisure, where time is not of the essence, relax with a few deep breaths, and while you are exhaling, stop in the middle of your exhale, with your lungs 50 percent full of oxygen (**figure 5.17A**). Take your shot during this short pause and then resume your exhale. The pause should not be held for more than ten seconds. After ten seconds, your muscles start to fatigue and your vision begins to blur due to lack of oxygen in the blood. Repeat this process for each shot until you find a rhythm to your shooting.

Alternatively, you can pause when you are finished exhaling and take your shot. Your body naturally pauses after an exhale for a few seconds. This is known as your natural respiratory pause, and it can be extended by holding your breath. During this period, make sure the handgun is not moving, and press the trigger (**figure 5.17B**).

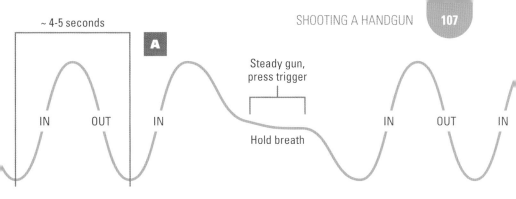

FIGURE 5.17. Learning to control your breathing is important to prevent handgun movement while you are shooting. **A.** A popular breath control technique is to hold your breath halfway through an exhale. After steadying the handgun, press the trigger and then continue to exhale. Each inhale/exhale cycle takes about 4–5 seconds. **B.** There is a natural respiratory pause after each exhale. You can hold your breath at one of these pauses, steady your handgun, and then press the trigger.

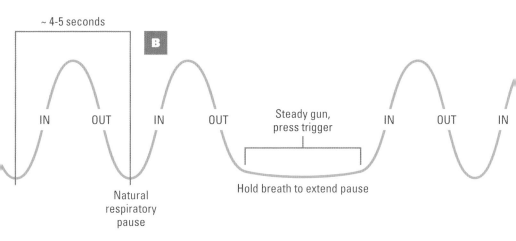

In a defensive or stressful situation, you will not have the time to consider your breathing pattern, or any of the fundamentals of shooting. You will default to muscle memory and the things that you have practiced.

5.2.1.1. Arc of Movement

While holding your breath, you have to steady the gun, make sure that the sights are aligned on target, and press the trigger, all while dealing with the natural movements of your body. Holding a weighted object, such as a handgun, out in front of your body is an atypical action, so your muscles will tire quickly and your hands will start to shake. Because of this, it is impossible to hold a handgun out in front of you without it moving; it will naturally sway, a motion known as its arc of movement. Breathing contributes to this, so holding your breath helps eliminate some of the movement.

When you are aligning the sights of the handgun, the arc of movement is high, since you are physically moving the handgun to get it properly positioned. Once your alignment is largely settled, your body begins to calm and the arc of movement lowers. It is during this

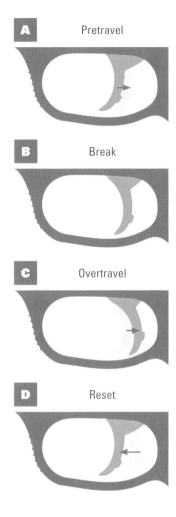

A. Pretravel

B. Break

C. Overtravel

D. Reset

FIGURE 5.18. There are multiple distinct phases associated with pressing a trigger. **A.** The pretravel phase consists of any rearward movement of the trigger until the hammer/striker is released. Depending on the firearm, this phase can be pronounced, or almost nonexistent. **B.** The break is the moment the hammer/striker is released and the gun is fired. **C.** Overtravel is any rearward movement of the trigger after the break. **D.** After completing the overtravel, the trigger resets, returning to its original position.

period of time that you want to press the trigger. If you wait too long, the arc of movement will begin to increase as your muscles tire from dwindling oxygen due to your held breath.

5.2.2. Trigger Control

It might not seem blatantly obvious, but how you press the trigger on a handgun has a significant impact on whether you hit what you are aiming at. This is known as trigger control. Depending on how you press the trigger, you could easily move the entire gun, not just the trigger. Articulating the trigger without imparting any additional movement on the handgun is more difficult than it sounds. Pressing a trigger is a simple idea in concept, but there is a lot that actually goes into the action, and understanding all these aspects will help you properly press one.

5.2.2.1. Phases of Pressing a Trigger

There are multiple distinct phases associated with pressing a trigger, which can be easily visualized by considering a retractable pen. When pressing the plunger on a retractable pen, there is preclick movement, the click, postclick movement, and the reset, where the plunger pops back to its original position. These same basic stages are present when pressing a trigger on a handgun (**figure 5.18**), albeit with different names: pretravel, break, overtravel, and reset.

1. Pretravel

All the movement of the trigger until the sear releases the hammer is called the pretravel (**figure 5.18A**). The sear is part of the trigger mechanism that keeps the hammer / spring-loaded striker in the cocked position. When the hammer / spring-loaded striker is cocked, tension is put on the mainspring, storing potential energy, ready to be released to fire the handgun.

2. Break

During the last portion of the pretravel phase, the trigger interacts with the sear and moves it to release the hammer/striker. The release of the hammer/striker is referred to as the break (**figure 5.18B**). Once the break occurs, there is no turning back; a cartridge is discharged.

3. Overtravel

After the break, the trigger does not simply stop. There is usually some additional rearward movement after the break. This is referred to as overtravel (**figure 5.18C**). This movement is stopped by the frame of the handgun, or by some other mechanical device attached to the back of the trigger. If this travel distance is pronounced, it can be easy to jerk the gun before the movement is complete, moving the gun and affecting the placement of the shot.

4. Reset
The final phase is the reset (**figure 5.18D**), where the trigger returns to its original position, reengaging the sear and preparing to fire another round.

5.2.2.2. Trigger Weight
Aside from just movement, there is a resistance associated with pressing the trigger, called the trigger weight. This is often measured in pounds and is colloquially known as the "trigger pull." When pressing a trigger, you will hit a rigid wall of resistance at the end of the pretravel phase. This is where the trigger engages the sear. Once the wall is overcome, the sear moves and releases the hammer/striker, which propels the firing pin into the primer of the loaded cartridge, setting off the charge and firing the gun.

How the trigger weight is distributed over the duration of pressing the trigger depends on the firearm. Some triggers have a noticeable pretravel, usually with a slowly increasing resistance leading to a marked increase in resistance before the break. Others are largely devoid of a pretravel, with just a wall of resistance before the break. Being aware of the phases associated with the trigger of your handgun, and how the resistance is distributed, is very important if you do not want to inadvertently move the gun while pressing the trigger.

5.2.2.3. Single-Action versus Double-Action Triggers
The trigger pull of a handgun is influenced by whether it has a single-action or a double-action trigger. Since the only job of a single-action trigger is to release the hammer/striker, such triggers often have fairly low, or "light," trigger pulls (about 2–3 pounds). Handguns with double-action triggers, however, generally have longer and heavier trigger pulls (about 10–15 pounds), since the trigger must set the hammer/striker and then release it.

As a general rule, it is easier to shoot a firearm with a lighter trigger pull. It is difficult to keep a lightweight handgun stable if you have to apply a significant amount of force to press the trigger. As an example, a double-action Ruger LCR .38 Special revolver weighs about 15 ounces (0.94 pounds) fully loaded and has a trigger pull of around 10 pounds. That is a sizable amount of force to apply to such a light handgun and keep the sights aligned on the target the entire time.

5.2.2.4. Finger Placement
The placement of your index finger on the trigger plays an important role in being able to properly press the trigger. The most widely accepted point of contact with the trigger is the pad of the distal segment (**figure 5.19A**). This position makes it easiest to move the trigger directly backward. If there is any sideward movement as you move the trigger, the amount of pressure required to press it increases (pulling straight backwards is the path of least resistance, and requires the least amount of pressure applied). Furthermore, that small amount of sideward pressure is enough to bring your sights out of alignment. If you find that your shots are veering to the left or right of where you intend, it likely has something to do with how you are pressing the trigger. If you contact the trigger with the tip of your finger (**figure 5.19B**), that usually imparts some leftward movement on the gun as you press the trigger (if you are shooting right-handed), resulting in your shots falling to the left of where you intended. If you contact the trigger at the joint between the distal two segments

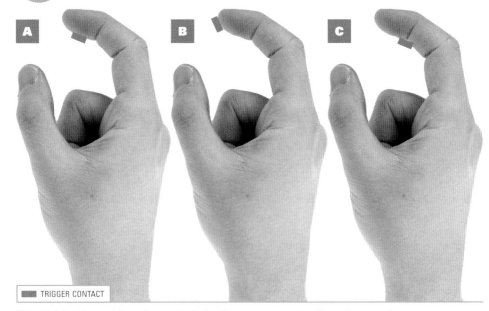

TRIGGER CONTACT

FIGURE 5.19. The position where your index finger contacts the trigger has an effect on your shot placement. **A.** When shooting a handgun, the trigger should contact the pad of your first digit. **B.** If the trigger contacts the edge of your finger tip, you will often add some leftward movement to the gun as your press the trigger (for right-handed shooters). This puts your shots to the left of where you were aiming. **C.** If the trigger contacts the joint between the distal two segments of your index finger, you will often add some rightward movement to the gun when you press the trigger (for right-handed shooters). This puts your shots to the right of where you were aiming. This trigger placement is used with heavier, double-action triggers found on magnum revolvers.

(**figure 5.19C**), you often have too much leverage on the trigger and will often pull the gun to the right as you press the trigger (if you are shooting right-handed). This trigger placement is used for double-action revolvers, which require more force to press the trigger. This gives you a little extra leverage to more easily handle the heavier trigger pull.

5.2.2.5. "Press" the Trigger

You may be wondering why the term "press" has been used in place of "pull" when talking about moving the trigger. While somewhat of an issue of semantics, "pulling" is an imprecise action. The word often conjures images of tugging a rope, an action that does not give you exacting control over the object you are moving. When moving the trigger of a handgun, you want it to be a very precise movement, one where only the trigger moves. This is not something that you get from "pulling." The action of "pressing" something is more exact, the sort of precision that you need when shooting a handgun. Noting this difference helps highlight the importance of not imparting additional movement on the handgun when moving the trigger.

When pressing the trigger of a handgun, you want to apply pressure slowly and evenly until the break occurs. Ideally, the break should come as a surprise. If you are anticipating the break, you may prematurely try to counteract the recoil, and thus jerk the gun, bringing the sights out of alignment. Anticipating the break and flinching is most often a problem associated with handguns with more-significant recoil. The shooter is anticipating the recoil and tries to brace for it, altering the sight picture before the gun is fired, or as it is being fired.

You can practice properly pressing the trigger of your handgun while it is unloaded. Balance a penny on the front sight of your handgun and practice pressing the trigger until you can do so without moving the gun and knocking the penny off (if your front sight is big enough to support a penny). Pressing the trigger on an unloaded gun is often referred to as "dry-firing." If you are going to be frequently dry-firing a gun, you should use dummy rounds (a plastic or aluminum round with no primer and no propellant) to prevent wear on the gun. With most firearms that shoot centerfire cartridges, dry-firing is relatively harmless. However, dry-firing a firearm that shoots rimfire cartridges is not recommended, since the firing pin will hit the rim of the empty chamber. If you are unsure about dry-firing your firearm, make sure to look in the owner's manual.

5.2.3. Follow-Through

The last aspect to consider when trying to avoid moving the gun while pressing the trigger is follow-through. Since pressing the trigger does not end with the break, your concentration should not end there. You need to follow through with your grip, stance, sight alignment, sight picture, and breathing. If you pull your eyes away from the sights after the break, or start to loosen your grip, the gun may move before the shot has fully left the gun, ensuring that you will not hit where you intended. Your gun tends to follow your eyes, so looking left or right before the shot is finished will undoubtedly cause you to miss your target. Everything you were doing before the break should be maintained after the break, until you reset the trigger. After the reset, you can move your head and assess where your shot hit the target.

The concept of follow-through is one that you can find in almost every sport. When someone is playing golf, they continue their swing after the ball is struck, to ensure that the ball stays on the course that they intend. The same exists with photography as well. If you start to move the camera before the shutter completes its cycle, your images will be blurry. Shooting a handgun is no different.

5.3. Additional Points to Improve Your Shooting

The two main tenets described in this chapter, and all the fundamentals that go with them, are what you need to follow to shoot a handgun successfully, regardless of the type. Beyond these things, there are a number of other points that deserve mention to improve your success at shooting.

5.3.1. Limit Your Round Count

When practicing at the shooting range, each time you step up to the line to shoot, you should limit your round count. Most semiautomatic handguns have magazines that hold more than five rounds, but loading more is counterproductive when you are practicing. It can be difficult to maintain your full concentration when shooting more than five rounds at a time. Even with five shots, shooters will often let up on their concentration on the last shot, thinking they are finished, and move the gun before the shot clears the gun.

FIGURE 5.20. When shooting a handgun, you should start practicing at shorter distances before shooting longer distances. In this picture, the shooter has the target 15 feet away, which is a good starting distance.

5.3.2. Practice Shooting Targets at a Distance of 7 Yards

Aside from limiting your round count when practicing, you should make sure that your targets are relatively close to you (**figure 5.20**). You want to be close enough to be able to see where your shots are hitting the target. You need to know where you are hitting, with respect to where you are aiming; otherwise you will not know how to start improving. A good starting distance would be 3 yards (9 feet / 2.7 meters) to 5 yards (15 feet / 4.6 meters), working up to 7 yards (21 feet / 6.4 meters).

If you ever need to use your handgun defensively, it will likely be at an extremely short range, so that is how you should practice, at least initially. If the threat is 25 yards away or more, you should be finding a means to escape that does not include shooting.

5.3.3. "Aim Small, Miss Small"

If you have seen Roland Emmerich's American Revolutionary War film *The Patriot*, you might remember Mel Gibson's character telling his sons to "Aim small, miss small" when shooting their rifles. This might seem counterintuitive, but on closer inspection the logic in it shows itself. If you are aiming at a large target, your eyes will try to focus on the entirety of it and falter, negatively affecting your aim (**figure 5.21A**). If you choose to aim at one small part of a target, you will be able to more successfully focus on it (**figure 5.21B**), and even if you don't hit it exactly, you will be in the vicinity. This mantra is applicable not only with shooting firearms, but also with archery and golf.

FIGURE 5.21. "Aim Small, Miss Small." **A.** If you are aiming at a large target, without something specific to focus on, it will be harder to hit where you intend. **B.** If you are aiming at a smaller target, with something specific to aim at, you will often be more successful.

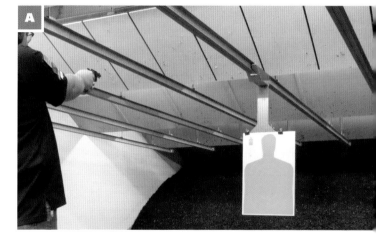

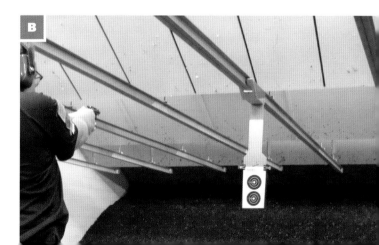

PATHWAY TO
SUCCESS

CHAPTER 6 PATHWAY TO SUCCESS

After becoming familiar with all the basics of shooting a handgun, you need to start practicing them. Just having a good grasp of the techniques discussed in this book is not enough to shoot well. The techniques must be practiced, such that you can perform them correctly and so they become second nature. Shooting a handgun is not a skill that comes naturally. Your body is not accustomed to holding a weighted object in front of you with your arms extended. Articulating your index finger individually, without moving your other digits, is not something that the hand evolved to do (it evolved for grasping). Because these things do not come naturally, practicing is essential to become proficient at shooting.

Frequently, problems with shooting arise from difficulties implementing the two tenets discussed in sections 5.1 and 5.2: presenting the pistol consistently, and not moving the gun when pressing the trigger. As obvious as it might seem, your target is the barometer for how well you are shooting. If your shots are not going where you are aiming, it is because you are inconsistent in your form, or you are moving the gun as you are pressing the trigger. Not all successful shooters use the grips and stances discussed in this book, but they all have found methods that work for them, methods that they are able to do consistently. If all your shots consistently go to the same place, even if it is not where you intended, a few changes in form can likely correct this. In this chapter, many common shooting errors are addressed, describing how they arise and how to correct them. Aside from accuracy problems, you could also run into mechanical malfunctions that could prevent you from shooting. This chapter discusses diagnosing mechanical problems and resolving them.

6.1. Make Sure You Are Close Enough to the Target

Before getting into specific shooting errors, you need to make sure that you are actually hitting some portion of the target that you are aiming at, and that you can see where your shots are going. If you cannot see the bullet holes on the target, then you are missing the entirety of the target. You will not gain any beneficial information about what you are doing if you cannot tell where your shots are going. If you are missing the target, you need to stand closer to the target until your shots hit the target. Once your shots are hitting the target, you can compare their placement to where you were aiming, and then work to correct it.

ASIDE: KENTUCKY WINDAGE

The goal of shooting is not to hit the center of the target, but rather to hit what you are aiming at. If you find that you are consistently hitting the target low and to the left, you might be inclined to simply aim a little higher and to the right in order to hit the center of the target. This is a poor solution to the problem, since you are sidestepping some error in your form/technique. This is sometimes referred to as "Kentucky windage." The name was derived from a practice used by marksmen on the American frontier, where they would aim to one side of their target to adjust for wind or movement rather than adjusting the sights on the gun. Practitioners used muzzle-loading long rifles, often called Kentucky Long Rifles, contributing to the name "Kentucky windage."

6.2. Shot Analysis

Unless all your shots are going exactly where you intend them to, you would benefit from analyzing where your shots are hitting the target. Comparing where you are hitting to where you are aiming can be informative. If your shots are not hitting where you are aiming, it is likely due to some error in the techniques discussed in chapter 5. Something that you are doing while firing, or slightly before, is moving the gun enough to bring your sights out of alignment. This section will be focused on some common shot placements and the errors that produce them. The shot placements to follow are described from the perspective of a right-handed shooter, but the concepts are the same for a left-handed shooter, just in reverse. It should also be noted that the following suggestions are not intended to be the final word on shooting errors and problems. They are merely a look at some common shot placements and what might cause them. These suggestions are to serve as a starting point for addressing problems that arise.

The shot analysis to follow is broken down into the quadrants of a circular target, with each region named on the basis of their geographical location, assuming the top of the target is north and the bottom is south. For each shot placement discussed, it is assumed that the shooter is aiming at the center of the target. Most of the described shot placements show someone who is very consistent, in that all their shots are going to the same general place, but their shots are not hitting where they were aiming (the center). As a shooter, this is a good position to be in,

ASIDE: AVOID ADJUSTING THE SIGHTS OF A NEW HANDGUN UNTIL YOU HAVE SHOT SEVERAL HUNDRED ROUNDS THROUGH IT.

After first purchasing a handgun, you should generally not adjust the sights right away. You need to practice with the gun and make sure that it is not your technique that is making your shots go somewhere other than where you intend them to go. It is to your benefit to be patient and make certain where the errors are coming from, before adjusting the gun sights only to discover you were at fault. It is also a good idea to have someone else shoot your gun and see if they have the same trouble. If they do not, and the gun is right on target, it is likely that you are doing something incorrectly.

since it means that they have largely accomplished the first tenet of shooting successfully: presenting the gun consistently. Once a shooter has established consistency, they likely need to change only one aspect of their technique to start hitting where they intend.

Southwest: If you find that all your shots are hitting in the southwest region of the target, it is likely that you are anticipating the motion of pulling the trigger and then jerking the trigger rather than smoothly pressing it. This jerking motion leads to the front sight dropping to the left before the bullet has cleared the barrel. If the gun has a significant recoil, you can experience a similar problem if you are anticipating the recoil and jerking the gun and the trigger, trying to prematurely counteract the kick. Even if a firearm has little to no recoil, a shooter can still anticipate the gun going off, and move the gun.

This shot placement can also result from having too tight of a grip on the handgun. You should always maintain a tight grip on the gun to avoid it lurching in your hand from the recoil, but if your grip with your right hand is too tight, it can angle the gun to the left.

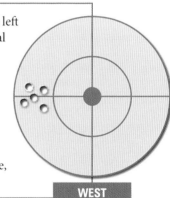

SOUTHWEST

West: If your shots are in line with the center, but off the left (west) side of the target, you may not be applying equal pressure from both hands and arms. If you are applying more force with your right hand than your left, you will often push the shots slightly to the left.

The same thing can happen if you do not have your finger on the trigger properly. Normally, the middle of the distal segment of your index finger should be contacting the trigger. If only the tip of your finger is contacting the trigger, you will pull the trigger at an angle, which will angle the front of the handgun to the left.

WEST

Northwest: If you find that all your shots are falling in the northwest quadrant of the target, you may not be following through with your shots properly. The most common variant of this is lifting your head up to see where your shot hit the target, but doing it too soon, such that the motion perturbs the gun as the bullet is leaving the barrel. Keep your head down and focused on the front sight of your gun until the shot has broken and fully left the gun.

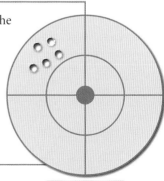

NORTHWEST

North: If you find that all your shots are hitting north of your point of aim, you could be aligning your sights improperly, with the front post rising above the notch of the rear sight. It can also result from not having your wrist locked, such that when the shot is fired, your wrist buckles upward from the recoil, altering the sight alignment before the bullet clears the barrel.

The same thing can also occur if are you anticipating the recoil of the gun and pushing forward on the handle before the gun fires, as a means to counteract the recoil. This is often called "heeling," since you are pushing forward with the heel of your hand. This motion will raise the front sight out of alignment as you are pressing the trigger.

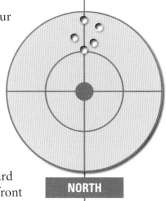

NORTH

Northeast: If your shots are landing northeast of the center of the target, it is likely due to "heeling," which was described above. In anticipation of the recoil, you push forward with the heel of your hand, right before the gun fires.

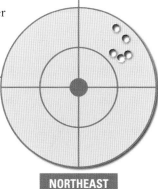

NORTHEAST

East: If your shots are off to the right of center (east), you might have too much of your index finger on the trigger. If your finger contacts the trigger at the joint between the distal two segments of your index finger, you have more leverage on the trigger than you need (unless you are shooting a double-action revolver). This will result in you pulling the trigger at an angle and moving the muzzle slightly to the right.

Sometimes this problem also results from applying too much pressure on the pistol handle or slide with your thumbs, which forces the muzzle of the gun to the right. The same thing could happen if you are applying too much force with your nonshooting hand.

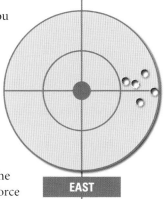

EAST

Southeast: If your shots are appearing in the southwest quadrant of the target, it suggests that you may be tightening your grip right before the shot fires. This causes the front sight to fall toward the right. It is important to always have a tight grip on the gun, but you want it to be consistently tight. If the tightness of your grip increases as you pull the trigger, you will bring the sights out of alignment.

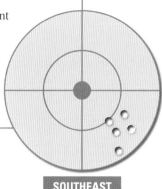

SOUTHEAST

South: If your shots are falling south of your point of aim, you could have a problem with sight alignment. If your front sight is buried within the notched rear sight, you will hit lower on the target than you intend. You want the top of the front sight to line up with the top of the notched rear sight, with the front sight evenly spaced between the sides of the notch.

Additionally, if you are anticipating the recoil of the gun, "heeling" can play a part in southward shot placement. In anticipation, you push the gun downward.

When you are shooting, you should always try to bring the gun up to your eyes and not drop your gaze down to line the sights with the target. If you are dropping your head, it could lead to your shots migrating below your point of aim, because your handgun will follow your eyes.

SOUTH

Everywhere: If your shots are spread across the entire target in a seemingly random array, it suggests that you need to work on the first tenet of shooting a firearm: presenting the gun consistently. Perhaps you have not settled on a grip on the handgun that suits you, or you are still experimenting with stances. Your first order of business is to get most of your shots in the same place, and then you can worry about making sure they are going exactly where you are intending them to go.

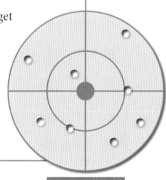

EVERYWHERE

6.3. Mechanical Malfunctions

Anyone who starts to seriously shoot handguns is going to run into malfunctions, regardless of how careful they are. These malfunctions are split between cartridge malfunctions (which were discussed in section 3.4.1) and mechanical malfunctions with the firearm itself. Most firearms produced today are manufactured with exacting standards, so mechanical failures are less common than they were with older firearms. Despite this, they still happen, some of which arise from poor shooting form. It is important to be aware of the common firearm malfunctions so that you can recognize them and resolve them when they come up.

6.3.1. Misfire

As discussed in section 3.4.1, a misfire occurs when the primer of a cartridge is dented, but the cartridge does not ignite and fire the bullet. This can be the result of a defective primer, but it can also be an issue with the firing pin of your handgun, where it does not strike the primer strongly enough. If you pull the trigger and a round does not fire, you should keep the gun pointed downrange for thirty seconds to see if it will go off. If it does not, unload the handgun while keeping it pointed in a safe direction. In the case of a semiautomatic pistol, first remove the magazine, then pull back the slide to eject the round in question. Inspect it to see if the primer is dented. If it is, try to shoot the cartridge a second time. If it still does not fire, there may be a problem with the primer. If the primer is only slightly dented, or not dented at all, there is likely an issue with the firing pin of your handgun, which will require the talents of a gunsmith to repair.

A

6.3.2. Stovepipe

A stovepipe occurs when a semiautomatic handgun fails to properly eject a spent cartridge. The empty casing is partially ejected from the chamber, but it does not fully clear the pistol (**figure 6.1A**). Oftentimes, as the slide moves forward to chamber a new cartridge, it

B

FIGURE 6.1. Anyone who does a lot of shooting should be aware of potential problems that could occur, some arising from mechanical malfunctions, and some from poor shooting form. **A.** A stovepipe is when the case of a fired cartridge does not properly get ejected and is caught in the slide as the handgun is chambering a new cartridge. **B.** Failure to go into battery is when a cartridge is not fully seated into the chamber.

catches the empty casing before it leaves the gun, which prevents the slide from properly closing. Stovepipes can result from a faulty extractor, but most frequently they are caused by the user not gripping the firearm firmly enough. You need to hold the frame firmly, such that the slide cycles back fully, building up sufficient energy to extract the empty case and then chamber a new round. With a weak grip, the gun will rock backward, moving with the slide, preventing the slide from cycling back fully. This is often referred to as "limp-wristing" and is a common problem for new shooters.

To resolve a stovepipe, remove the magazine from the gun and then pull back the slide to allow the empty case to fall to the floor. Once the empty case has been removed, insert the magazine again, chamber a new round by pulling back the slide, and get back to shooting.

6.3.3. Failure to Go into Battery

In some instances, the slide of a semiautomatic handgun might not fully go forward, stopping before the cartridge is fully seated into the chamber. This is referred to as failure to go into battery (**figure 6.1B**). This can be dangerous if the firearm is able to fire, since the buildup of pressure could rupture the case if it is not properly supported by the chamber.

Because of potential problems like this, it is important to be very aware of what is happening with your gun with every shot. If you notice that the slide has not fully cycled forward, you should remove the magazine of the gun. Then, with the muzzle pointed downrange, pull back the slide to eject the cartridge that was not seated properly. Examine the ejected round; if it looks normal, put it back into the magazine and try firing it again. If the problem persists, it may be because your handgun needs to be cleaned. If you do not properly clean your handgun, dirt and gunpowder residue can build up and prevent all the mechanisms from functioning smoothly.

Failure to go into battery can also happen with a new firearm that has hardly been used. Most firearms function best after they have been shot extensively, and the parts have worn a little. Usually, a firearm will be functioning its best after a few hundred rounds have been cycled through it.

Another cause for failure to go into battery is if you keep your fingers on the slide when you release it, in an attempt to gently drop the slide. The friction of your fingers against the slide can prevent it from fully inserting a cartridge into the chamber. This is often referred to as "riding the slide." The slide of a handgun is designed to close from its fully retracted position unimpeded. Furthermore, depending on the grip that you adopt on your handgun, your thumbs might be pressing up against the slide. This contact can lead to the same problems that riding the slide causes. On some rare occasions, a cartridge might not meet the proper dimensions to fit into the gun, due to an error in manufacturing that bypassed quality control. If the cartridge does not properly fit into the chamber, it will prevent gun from going into battery.

6.3.4. Double Feed

A double feed occurs in a semiautomatic handgun when a cartridge is still in the chamber but the slide attempts to push a new round into it. This can occur with a live round in the chamber, or with an empty case. If there is a problem with the extractor of the gun, and the empty case is not removed after firing a round, when the gun goes to load a new round into the chamber it will be pushed into the empty case. In the instance of a faulty extractor, the handgun should be taken to a gunsmith for inspection and repair. If a double feed occurs with a live round already in the chamber, it is likely a problem with the magazine that the gun is using, since it is allowing the slide to attempt to put two rounds into the chamber.

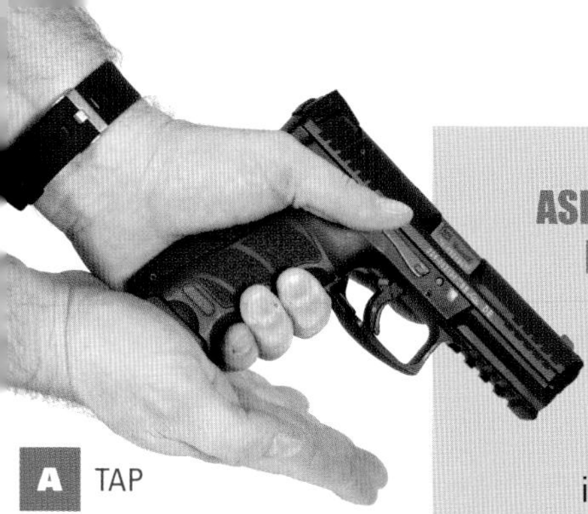

A TAP

FIGURE 6.2. Tap, rack, and go is a quick and effective way to get your handgun functioning after a misfire or stovepipe. **A.** As a first step, tap the magazine of your handgun and make sure it is properly inserted. **B.** As a second step, pull back the slide to eject the misfired cartridge or caught case. The slide will move forward and load a new cartridge into the chamber. **C.** As a third step, your firearm is loaded and ready to fire. You are ready to go.

B RACK

C GO

ASIDE: CLEARING MISFIRES IN A DEFENSIVE SITUATIONS

If a problem arises while you are trying to defend yourself, you will not have the time to wait for thirty seconds to see if you have a misfire, nor will you have time to carefully investigate what is amiss. Such situations require immediate action. A widely used strategy for clearing a semiautomatic pistol is "tap, rack, and go," its name derived from the actions associated with the technique.

Tap, rack, and go is effective for many common problems, such as defective ammunition or improperly seated magazines. The technique is as follows:

1. **TAP:** Use your nonshooting hand to "tap" the base of magazine to make sure it is properly inserted. Sometimes a handgun will fail to fire because the magazine is not fully inserted, such that the cartridge cannot properly feed into the chamber. While it is called a "tap," you should put more force into it than simply a light tap (**figure 6.2A**).

2. **RACK:** Pull the slide back on your handgun. This will eject whatever round is in the chamber and feed a new cartridge into the chamber (**figure 6.2B**).

3. **GO:** Now you are ready to fire your handgun again. If it still does not fire, there is likely a larger problem with your handgun, and you should seek cover to investigate what is wrong (**figure 6.2C**).

Tap, rack, and go is not a fix for all potential problems. If you have a squib trapped in the barrel of your handgun, tap, rack, and go is dangerous. Since a bullet is trapped in the barrel of your handgun, tap, rack, and go would result in you firing another round into the one trapped in the barrel. Squib rounds are not very common and usually occur only with reloaded ammunition. Because of this, you should always use factory-loaded ammunition for your defensive handgun.

FIGURE 6.3. In order to make sure your firearms function flawlessly, you should clean them regularly. Pictured is a shooting enthusiast carefully cleaning his handgun and making sure that it is properly lubricated.

ASIDE: HOW OFTEN SHOULD YOU CLEAN YOUR HANDGUN?

After firing a handgun, dirt and gunpowder residue will gather in the barrel and working mechanisms of the firearm. Firearms need to be properly lubricated with oil to function well, though that oil has a tendency to collect dirt. If you let the dirt and debris accumulate, it will begin to affect the firearm's reliability. It is important that you clean your firearms and keep them lubricated if you want them to function properly (**figure 6.3**).

Should you clean your firearm after every time you have it at the range? This is a topic that people have wildly different opinions about. Some individuals clean their guns after every time that they fire them. Still others are not concerned with cleaning their guns, figuring that their guns will let them know when they need to be cleaned (i.e., when they start to malfunction). It is worth checking the owner's manual of your handgun to see what the manufacturer suggests for maintenance. Cleaning your handgun after every range visit might be more than necessary, especially if you plan to be back at the range within a day or two. But waiting until your gun is so dirty that it starts to malfunction is not the most auspicious choice either.

CONCLUDING REMARKS

Due to their potential to cause serious bodily harm, firearms need to be treated with respect. With the information in this book, you should have all the knowledge you need to comfortably handle firearms safely and effectively.

Safety Is Key

Of all the information presented in this book, learning proper firearms safety is the most critical. The three rules of gun safety are ones that cannot be overstated:

1. A firearm should never be pointed at someone or cross over any part of a person.
You should never point a firearm at yourself or another person, unless you are prepared to shoot them. This might seem obvious, but just knowing the rule is not the same as internalizing it. The moment something goes slightly amiss, such as when you have a misfire, it is very easy to forget where the muzzle is pointing as you are trying to resolve the problem. A handgun is small and relatively easy to point at yourself or another person inadvertently. It can be helpful to imagine that the muzzle of your handgun has a laser pointer on it. You need to make certain that no part of that laser ever passes over your body or that of another person.

2. Treat all firearms as if they are loaded.
Every time that you pick up a handgun, you should handle it as if it were loaded. You would not want to point a loaded handgun at a friend, so you should not point an unloaded firearm at a friend. Just because you know that it is unloaded does not mean that everyone else knows that information. Furthermore, loading a cartridge into the chamber of the gun can be done in an instant, perhaps unbeknownst to you if someone else handled it before you.

On top of assuming that every handgun is loaded, every time you handle one, you should physically check to see if it is loaded. This should become a habit every time you pick up a gun. Even if someone else checked the gun before handing it to you, you still need to check it yourself by looking inside the chamber to ensure that a cartridge is not inserted. Doing so is not suggesting that you do not trust them, it is you practicing safe gun-handling skills.

3. Your finger should never be on the trigger until you are ready to shoot.
Whenever you are handling a firearm, you should keep your finger off the trigger until you are prepared to shoot it. You should place your index finger somewhere on the frame of the gun, not the trigger guard. Having your finger on the trigger prematurely could lead to you firing the gun accidentally, especially if it has a light trigger pull.

How to Effectively Shoot a Handgun

Once you know how to handle a gun safely, your attention can be focused on learning to shoot effectively. While many disparate elements go into shooting a handgun, you can simplify the whole process into two key tenets: present the pistol consistently and then do not move the gun when pressing the trigger.

Learning to be consistent is extremely important if you want to shoot well. If you adopt a different grip on the handgun every time you pick it up, that variability is going to show up in your shot placement on the target. Because of this, you want to make sure every finger of your shooting hand has a defined place on the gun. Your second hand should be in a position where it adds support to the gun. Ideally, you want to be pushing forward with your shooting hand and pulling backward with your second hand. This "push and pull" dynamic helps support the gun and keeps it from moving due to recoil.

Consistency in your stance is important as well. An effective stance provides a stable platform for shooting. Changes in stance will often result in inconsistency on the target. The Weaver and isosceles stances are some of the most widely used. Both stances put your feet at shoulder width apart, with a slight bend in the knees. The Weaver position places your nondominant foot slightly ahead of your dominant foot, whereas the isosceles position has both feet aligned. Both these placements are steady and well balanced, helping to avoid introducing any unnecessary movement. For arm placement, the Weaver position has your shooting arm straight and your other arm bent at the elbow, angled toward the ground. The isosceles position has both arms straight, forming what looks like an isosceles triangle from above. Each of these positions allows you to push forward with your shooting hand and pull backward with your other hand, helping to keep the gun stationary when shooting.

A consistent grip and stance will only go so far if you do not have a consistent sight alignment and sight picture. The front sight should be placed evenly between the sides of notch of the rear sight, with the top of the front sight aligned with the top of the rear sight. Sight picture is different for every handgun and has to be determined by experimentation. You might have to situate what you want to hit right above the front sight, or maybe you need to cover it with the post of the front sight. Once your sight alignment and sight picture are established, you need to focus specifically on the front sight, such that the target and rear sight blur slightly. It is impossible to focus on all three things at once, so you need to choose one.

Even if you are able to consistently present the gun, all of that will be thrown off if you move the handgun inadvertently while you press the trigger. Not moving the gun when pressing the trigger is the second tenet of shooting effectively.

Learning to control your breathing will help minimize the amount of movement it imparts on your shooting. The rise and fall of your chest while breathing can easily disrupt your sight alignment. A good solution to this is to take a few relaxed deep breaths and then pause in the middle of your exhale to steady the gun and press the trigger, before finishing the exhale.

How you press the trigger can have a significant impact on how successful you are at shooting. If you are not careful, you can impart movement on the gun while pressing the trigger. Ideally, you want to smoothly press the trigger in one fluid motion and be surprised by the break. Anticipating the recoil can lead to premature jerking motions that upset your sight alignment.

Another important thing to consider to avoid inadvertently moving your handgun is your follow-through. Your concentration should not end as soon as the shot breaks. After the break, there is a short period of time before the bullet completely leaves the barrel. If you lift your head to see where the shot lands before the bullet completely clears the barrel, you will disrupt your sight alignment and the shot will not go where you intended it.

Hours of Enjoyment Await You

Shooting can be an entertaining and rewarding pastime. There is nothing quite like the satisfaction of landing five shots in one tight group at the center of the target. Becoming a competent shooter is not something that will happen overnight. It has to be formed from lots of practice and dedication. If you follow the tenets laid out here, you will have an excellent foundation to build on, allowing you to make the most out of each of your practice sessions. If you treat firearms and other shooters with the respect they deserve, you will find that shooting is an enthralling hobby and one that can provide you with countless hours of enjoyment.

Practice sessions are a good way to develop friendships with like-minded shooters. They provide an excellent opportunity to improve your shooting skills by sharing ideas and techniques with others in a friendly environment.